Transport Curiosities, 1850–1950

Other books by John Wade

Cameras at War: Photo Gear that Captured 100 Years of Conflict – from Crimea to Korea (Pen & Sword, 2020)

The Golden Age of Science Fiction: A Journey into Space with 1950s Radio, TV, Films, Comics and Books (Pen & Sword, 2019)

London Curiosities: The Capital's Odd & Obscure, Weird & Wonderful Places (Pen & Sword, 2017)

The Ingenious Victorians: Weird and Wonderful Ideas from the Age of Innovation (Pen & Sword, 2016)

Transport Curiosities, 1850–1950

Weird and Wonderful Ways of Travelling by Road, Rail, Air and Sea

John Wade

PEN & SWORD
TRANSPORT

First published in Great Britain in 2022 by
Pen & Sword Transport
An imprint of
Pen & Sword Books Ltd
Yorkshire – Philadelphia

ISBN 978 1 39900 397 1

A CIP catalogue record for this book is
available from the British Library.

Printed and bound in the UK by CPI Group (UK) Ltd,
Croydon, CR0 4YY.

Pen & Sword Books Limited incorporates the imprints of Atlas, Archaeology,
Aviation, Discovery, Family History, Fiction, History, Maritime, Military,
Military Classics, Politics, Select, Transport, True Crime, Air World, Frontline
Publishing, Leo Cooper, Remember When, Seaforth Publishing, The Praetorian
Press, Wharncliffe Local History, Wharncliffe Transport, Wharncliffe True
Crime and White Owl.

For a complete list of Pen & Sword titles please contact

PEN & SWORD BOOKS LIMITED
47 Church Street, Barnsley, South Yorkshire, S70 2AS, England
E-mail: enquiries@pen-and-sword.co.uk
Website: www.pen-and-sword.co.uk

Or

PEN AND SWORD BOOKS
1950 Lawrence Rd, Havertown, PA 19083, USA
E-mail: Uspen-and-sword@casematepublishers.com
Website: www.penandswordbooks.com

Contents

Introduction

I magine you are standing on a railway platform, waiting for the next train to arrive. When one pulls into the station it is driven, surprisingly, by a team of horses. They are trotting without actually going anywhere because they are tethered to a treadmill that turns the wheels that propel this strange train. Not ready to believe your eyes, you turn to another platform where a second train speeds past without stopping, this one driven by a huge aircraft-like propeller fixed to the back. It is followed by what appears to be a normal car, running along the railway tracks.

Outside the station, a car drives past heading for the river at the end of the road, into which the driver plunges his vehicle to continue his journey by water, the back wheels of his car now acting as paddles. Meanwhile, across the road, the driver of a small car with huge rotating blades above the body attempts to take off and fly over the rooftops. Just as well he can't get his vehicle too high off the ground, otherwise he might collide with the aeroplane passing over with flapping wings.

This strangely surreal view of the world illustrates the way transport might have developed if just some of the many weird and wonderful ideas envisaged in the past had come to fruition.

Over the following pages, you will find not only railway engines driven by horses, but also the surprising number of cars, boats and trains that were driven by aeroplane propellers. Here you will discover cars that flew in the air or floated on water and boats that ran on roads; steam-powered aeroplanes, electric submarines, railways driven by pneumatic air, huge aircraft in which the passengers travelled in the wings ... and a whole lot more.

The years under consideration here are principally 1850 to 1950. However, the final years of this timeline were marked by the outbreak of the Second World War in 1939 and its continuation until 1945. The war marked a milestone in which transport of all types came of age. The basic methods of road, rail, air and sea transportation were now in place. They could be improved upon, but there was little more of the sideways thinking kind of experimentation that had so often previously led to weird and wonderful curiosities. Inventors and designers had no need to look at methods of getting an aircraft into the air and keeping it there, or of driving a car along a road, or a train along its tracks. Instead, they improved on what had become the norm. So while this book touches on the 1940s and dips a toe into the 1950s, it is mainly concerned with the earlier years in which delightful eccentricity was at the heart of so many modes of transport.

If you are a person who would like to have flown in an airship, or travelled in a train whose carriage sat on stilts above the sea with its tracks below the water, or might have dreamed of riding on a train whose journey from London to New York took twelve days to travel the long way round the world, or maybe just fancied fixing your bicycle to a railway track, then read on. It's time to meet an amazing group of inventors, designers, drivers, riders, flyers and sailors from the past, some of whose endeavours ended in success, but so many of whom sadly travelled only on the road to obscurity.

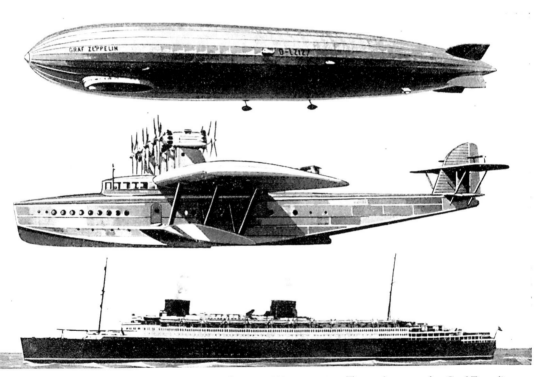

The future of international transportation from a 1929 viewpoint. Top to bottom: the *Graf Zeppelin* airship, the 100-seater Dornier seaplane driven by twelve engines, and the steamship *Bremen*, which was known for its ocean-going record-breaking speed.

Part I

Travel on Tracks

Sir Isaac Newton, the famous English mathematician, physicist, astronomer, theologian and author, designed a type of steam locomotive in 1690. Even so, it's widely accepted that railways didn't come to prominence until the nineteenth century. The earliest years of the era were epitomised by an engine called the *Rocket*, built for the Rainhill Trials of the Liverpool and Manchester Railways in 1829, which it won. It wasn't the first steam-powered railway engine, but it was probably the first to attain a measure of renown. The *Rocket*'s designer was civil and mechanical engineer George Stevenson, who became known as the Father of Railways. In the years that followed, many varied, sometimes unusual and often weird means of rail transport emerged. What follows are some of the best, the worst, the strange and the downright crazy ideas with which railway pioneers over the years have famously succeeded and spectacularly failed.

What Isaac Newton's steam engine might have looked like if it had been built.

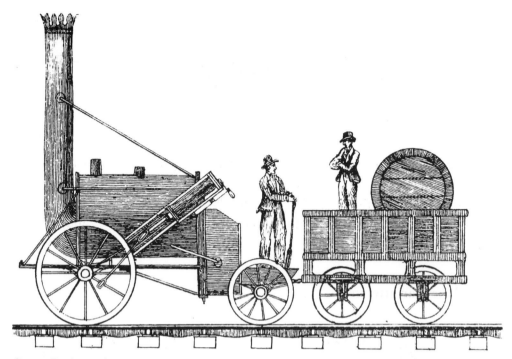

George Stephenson's *Rocket*, probably the first steam engine to gain public recognition.

Trains with Propellers

Using a propeller mounted on a carriage to drive it along a railway track might seem strange, but schemes for this unusual method of transport emerged, were abandoned and resurfaced a surprising number of times during the late nineteenth and early twentieth centuries. For a while, the idea of propeller-driven trains proliferated in many different countries.

Early American attempts

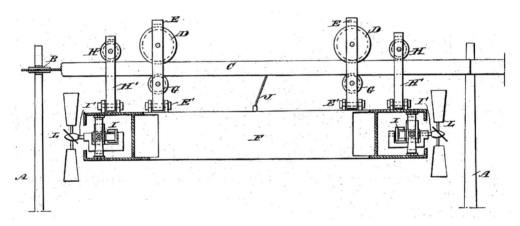

Anders Anderson's patent drawings for a propeller-driven train.

American inventor Anders Anderson was granted a patent for a propeller-driven monorail in 1892. In his patent, Anderson described a new and improved elevated railway which he claimed was simple and durable in construction. It was a time when monorail systems had begun to gain popularity, but mainly to transfer goods rather than people. Anderson's invention consisted of a fairly traditional looking railway carriage which, instead of running on tracks, was suspended from a wooden rail. It was driven by a propeller at each end of the carriage, most likely to have been run by one of the newly invented automobile engines. The propeller could be adapted to be thrown into any desired position to regulate the speed of the car. This, Anderson claimed, permitted convenient regulation of the speed of the carriage, while reducing friction to a minimum.

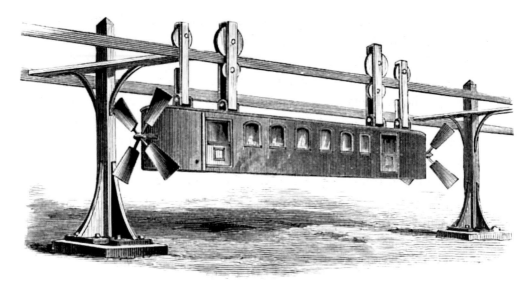

Anderson's propeller-driven train, pictured in *Scientific American* magazine.

A picture, published in a contemporary copy of *Scientific American* magazine, showed a long carriage with square ends, suspended from a rail by four pulley wheels and with a propeller, similar to those seen on aircraft of the time, at each end. There is little to indicate that Anderson's railway was ever built. But some years later, a second American gave it another go with the launch of an experimental monorail built in Burbank.

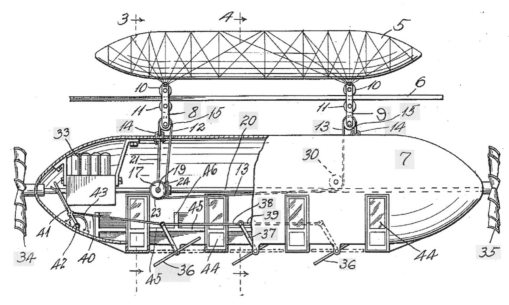

Joseph Fawkes's patent drawing for an aerial trolley car, the vehicle that became the Aerial Swallow.

The inventor this time was Joseph Fawkes and his propeller-driven railway was called the Aerial Swallow. It was shaped like a long, thin torpedo, suspended from an overhead iron rail using a gyroscope to balance it. Fawkes reckoned it could travel over roads, across ravines, streams and rivers with a claimed speed of up to 150 miles per hour. It never happened. The only journeys made by a prototype carriage were on a track through Fawkes's own orchard, enjoyed by a brave number of passengers between 1910 and 1912. When proposals were put forward to link Burbank with the centre of Los Angeles, Fawkes suggested building a line for his propeller-driven trains. His idea was turned down and a more conventional railway line was built. After this, the public lost interest and the Aerial Swallow was eventually left to rot in Fawkes's orchard. It became known by the public as Fawkes's Folly.

Fawkes's Aerial Swallow prototype, which eventually became known as Fawkes's Folly.

French devices

Meanwhile in France, inventor Francis Laur was having his own thoughts about propeller-driven railways with a vehicle he called the Aerial Monoflyer. In a patent filed in 1915 he described his idea for a 'vehicle for use in high-speed locomotion'. Once again, a single carriage was involved, but this one was egg-shaped to make it more aerodynamic. Propellers were mounted on the carriage, which even had short, stubby wings, designed to lift it slightly in the way wind under the wings of an aircraft lift it into the air. The Aerial Monoflyer's wings, however, were there only to lift it a little, relieving the tracks of some of the vehicle's weight, while at the same time allowing for what the inventor called 'guided flight'. The carriage straddled its monorail track, from which it drew an electric current to drive the propellers.

What the Aerial Monoflyer might have looked like.

A cover picture from *Le Petit Journal* magazine shows Francis Laur's proposals for the propeller-driven Aérocar.

An artist's impression of how it might look crossing a river on its overhead rails appeared in *Popular Science* magazine, with an editorial comment that showed a good deal of scepticism about its practicality.

Undeterred, Laur came up with a new idea for what he called the Aérocar, this time hanging from, rather than straddling, an overhead track suspended between towers similar to those of a more traditional suspension bridge. An artist's impression of what the Aérocar might have looked like appeared on the December 1924 cover of a French magazine called *Le Petite Journal*, where it was reported that consideration was being given to building a 1.86-mile length of working track to test the vehicle.

In 1928, work began in Germany for a revolutionary monorail service planned to eventually link Berlin with the Ruhr Valley. It featured streamlined torpedo-shaped carriages driven by propellers at each end originally designed for airships. The monorail was estimated to be capable of speeds of up to 200 miles per hour, nearly twice that of then current passenger-carrying aeroplanes and about four times that of a traditional railway engine. The cars would be hung on ball bearing rollers from an overhead track and electric motors would drive the propellers with power taken from an electrified rail. The cars for **the** system were designed by airship engineers.

Preliminary sketch of the proposed German monorail.

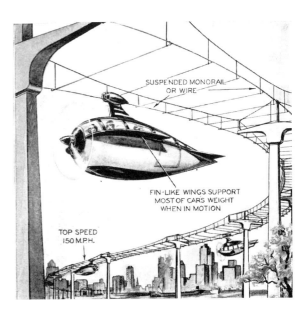

A streamlined German rail plane driven by a rear propeller.

Joseph Archer's air trolley.

Around the same time, another German rail car was proposed, driven this time by a propeller at the rear end of the body and a 400-horsepower aeroplane engine.

In May 1930, *Modern Mechanix* magazine reported on an idea for small, family-size carriages called Electric Air Trolleys from French inventor Joseph Archer. Each carriage was suspended from a track, from which it picked up an electric current to drive the propeller. Reversing the propeller would then bring it to a stop. Like the Aérocar, Archer's vehicle had small wings that helped support its weight and it was reckoned that it would be capable of travelling at 150 miles per hour.

A Russian locomotive

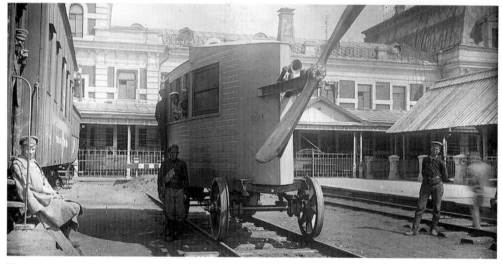

Valerian Abakovsky's Aerowagon.

Earlier in Russia, moves had been afoot for a propeller-driven railway, this time with a carriage that ran on conventional railway tracks. The idea came from inventor Valerian Abakovsky in 1917 with what he called an Aerowagon, designed to carry Soviet officials to and from Moscow. It comprised a carriage with an aeroplane propeller attached to an aeroplane engine. On its initial test run, it worked well, but retuning along the same route, it derailed, crashed and killed Abakovsky with four other passengers.

German designs

Two years later, German inventor Otto Steinitz patented another propeller-driven carriage that ran on normal railway tracks. He called it the Dringos Prop-Locomotive. Built from a railway freight wagon, it contained an aeroplane engine

Otto Steinitz (third from left) with his Dringos Prop-Locomotive.

to drive the propeller. In May 1919 it carried a party of German members of parliament and railway officials on a trip of about 30 miles and back at speeds of up to 60 miles per hour. It was reputed to have been very noisy. The idea was never taken any further.

Later, in 1930, also in Germany, came the debut of perhaps the most successful propeller-driven railway from Europe. It was called the Schienenzeppelin or Rail Zeppelin, due to its similarity to the Zeppelin airship. Even though it didn't get much further than the prototype stage, on a journey from Hamburg to Berlin it attained a speed of 143 miles per hour, a record it held for twenty years. It was built by engineer and railway pioneer Franz Kruckenberg, using a twin six-cylinder aircraft petrol engine to drive a rear-mounted, four-bladed propeller and accommodated forty passengers. The Rail Zeppelin was never put into full service.

The Rail Zeppelin at Hannover Station in Germany.

Few, if any, of these early attempts at building practical, working propeller-driven railways were ultimately successful. The one that came closest to commercial success was the Railplane, built in the UK by inventor George Bennie, who abandoned the idea of running his locomotive on traditional railway tracks and reverted to the earlier designs of suspending it from an overhead monorail

The Bennie Railplane

George Bennie was born in 1891, the son of John Bennie, owner of a hydraulic engineering company in Glasgow. As a young man, Bennie showed an ability to invent things that included new types of golf clubs, and he registered several patents. He had his first ideas for an unusual form of transport in the 1920s when he began to examine the plausibility of using wind power rather than steam to drive a railway engine. Furthermore, he saw the advantages of getting his railway running on rails suspended above the ground. In this way, it would not be affected by other traffic and, with the track built above a traditional railway line, it would be cost effective while lessening impact on the environment. Run purely as a passenger service, it also meant that passengers would not be affected or delayed by freight trains running on the same lines. Out of this thinking came the Railplane.

Bennie's original patent indicated that early plans were to run two carriages side by side, although when built, the tracks only carried one. In putting his plans forward Bennie was swift to explain the advantages of his Railplane over a more traditional railway line. To build such a line in the usual way meant clearing and

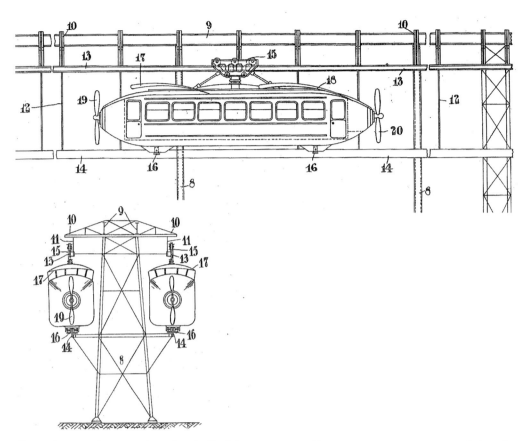

Bennie's patent drawings show that the Railplane was originally meant to run two carriages side by side on twin tracks.

levelling the track, building embankments and bridges and tunnelling though hills or other obstructions. The Railplane would ride above all of this. Also, by building the Railplane track over existing railway tracks or roads, money would be saved because it meant no new land needed to be purchased. It required only concrete pylons to be driven into the ground and spaced out over the length of one overhead track with a second track beneath.

An early artist's impression of the Railplane, published in the *Glasgow Herald* as early as 1921, showed the overhead tracks weaving across the countryside, across rivers and over hills, side by side with a traditional railway that needed bridges and tunnels to travel the same route.

All this came at a time when people were beginning to turn away from steam as a motive power and to look more seriously at the capabilities of the internal combustion engine and electricity. It was also a time when flying began to appear more practical than in the past and anything with a propeller looked exciting and new age.

On display at the Kelvingrove Museum, George Bennie's own model of the Railplane.

In 1929, Bennie was given permission to build a test track at Milngavie near Glasgow, running it above an existing branch line of the London and North Eastern Railway. The track ran for 426 feet, including a station where passengers could alight. The Railplane's propeller-driven carriage was built by the Scottish William Beardmore Company, a manufacturer of steam railway engines and road vehicles that included London taxis, as well as airships. Included among the latter was the famous R34 airship, the first to make a double crossing of the Atlantic in 1919.

The Railplane was made of aluminium on a wooden frame and took the shape of a cylinder 52 feet long, 8 feet wide and 8 feet high. There were driving compartments at each snub-nosed end, on which were mounted 9-foot diameter propellers. The test vehicle's propellers were electrically driven, but petrol engine drives were also considered. In the passenger compartment, the Railplane was far more luxurious than a railway carriage of the time. It had sliding access doors incorporating ornamental stained-glass panels made by Pilkington, comfortable plush seats designed by Waring and Gillow that were more like armchairs, electric lighting along its length, small semi-circular tables between the seats with electric lamps on them, a patterned carpet, panelled ceiling and curtains that could be drawn across wide windows. The test carriage had about twenty-four seats, although there were plans for larger seating capacities in future versions.

Early trials with the Railplane in 1929.

How the Railplane test track ran above an existing railway line.

The Railplane hung from the overhead track by means of bogies on its roof. On its underside, guide wheels ran along the second track to prevent the carriage from swaying during its journey or, worse still, swinging out on bends. In this way, Bennie reckoned his Railplane could accelerate to 60 miles per hour within 600 feet and attain a top speed of 120 miles per hour, at a time when the average aircraft was capable of little more than 100 miles per hour. Because of the carriage's aerodynamics, it would begin to support its own weight at around 100 miles per hour. Slowing down and breaking were effected by reversing the propellers and, when stationary, manually operated breaks gripped the rail to keep the carriage from moving when, for example, loading passengers.

The test track was opened on 8 July 1930, initially for visiting dignitaries, but then to any member of the public for the price of one shilling (5p) a trip. First impressions were favourable. Railway companies showed an interest because of the lower cost of building a Railplane system as against a traditional railway. It was also seen as the ideal method of transport across crowded cities where it was impractical to build normal railway lines and too costly to consider underground options.

Bennie had plans and generated interest for Railplane tracks connecting Stonebridge Park station in north-west London to the British Empire Exhibition taking place at Wembley. A Central London proposal would have seen a Railplane terminal at Marble Arch with tracks running over and above the traffic in Oxford Street to terminate at Croydon Airport. Another plan saw the possibility of Railplanes connecting new towns then being built in Essex during a time of slum

The Railplane in the station area of the test track.

Inside the Railplane carriage: George Bennie, standing, with fellow passengers.

How the Railplane was advertised in 1929.

clearance. There were plans for lines connecting London and Brighton, London and Dover, Brighton and Eastbourne, and Blackpool and Southport. A combined Railplane and sealink was considered for connecting London to Paris and Brussels. There was also talk of Railplane tracks being built in places like Africa, where an overhead system would be more practical than traditional railways for crossing deserts, and in the Middle East, where it was suggested it could be used to convey weekend tourists from Jerusalem to Tel Aviv or the Dead Sea.

Over the best part of a decade, proposals were considered and abandoned for numerous Railplane lines. The outbreak of the Second World War in 1939 put everything on hold, but following the war, there were half-hearted attempts to resurrect the Railplane. The French government considered building a track in Algeria and across the Sahara Desert, but nothing came of it. In 1950, Bennie visited Syria and Iraq to discuss the possibility of a 700-mile system to connect various cities. Proposals for lines in Los Angeles and Amsterdam were also suggested. Sadly, none of it ever came to fruition.

After a somewhat nomadic later life, George Bennie died relatively unknown, at a residential home in Surrey, in 1957.

Work begins on breaking up the Railplane for scrap in 1956.

The year before, in 1956, the Railplane's test track was torn down and sold for scrap. Today a builder's yard stands on its remains. A blue plaque, erected by Bearsden and Milngavie District Council and placed on a wall beside a main road close to the site, proclaims:

> To commemorate George Bennie's Railplane which was tested here on 8th July 1930. The bullet-shaped carriage with a propeller at each end was reputed to be the forerunner of the modern monorail. It was suspended from a single rail on a 426ft long purpose-built test track 30 feet above the former LNER railway line, situated to the east of this plaque.

Below this brief dissertation there is a crude representation of what the Railplane looked like. Above is George Bennie's name and the dates 1892–1957. The plaque maker got Bennie's birthdate wrong!

The plaque that today commemorates George Bennie's Railplane.

Pneumatic and Atmospheric Railways

While steam and electricity have always been the more popular methods of driving locomotives along tracks, there was a time when pneumatic air power seemed it might prove to be the next big thing in motive power.

Early experiments

In May 1861, at Battersea in south-west London, a cast-iron tube, 452 yards long, in the shape of a traditional railway tunnel but only 2 feet 9 inches high and varying between 2 feet 4 inches and 2 feet 6 inches wide, was laid along the south bank of the river Thames. Inside the tube, raised ledges 2 inches wide and 1 inch high formed crude tracks for a small, elongated capsule-like carriage that stood at the mouth of the tube. At the far end, a steam engine was set up to drive a huge flywheel. The capsule was introduced to one end of the tube and the steam engine

The experimental pneumatic railway test at Battersea.

set in motion. The flywheel, acting like a fan, created a vacuum in the tube which resulted in the capsule at the opposite end being 'sucked' along the interior. The journey took about thirty seconds. Although the idea had been proposed before and minor trials had been held near Birmingham, this was the first time a full-scale experiment had been planned to show the effectiveness of a pneumatic railway.

The initial use foreseen for a pneumatic railway was for the transport of gravel and other materials. But the fact that the capsules, while not high enough for anyone to sit in comfortably, were quite capable of carrying a man lying down, proved too much of a temptation for workmen on site not to risk a journey or two. Once demonstrations of this new and novel way of driving a carriage were seen by the pubic, more and more were willing to take the risk of making a journey. Three months after those initial trials in Battersea, the *Illustrated London News* carried a short announcement that stated:

> One trip was made in 60 seconds, and a second in 55 seconds. Two gentlemen occupied the carriages during the first trip. They lay on their backs on mattresses with horsecloths for covering, and appeared to be perfectly satisfied with their journey.

London Pneumatic Despatch Company

One of the earliest bodies to see the advantages of a pneumatic railway was the London Pneumatic Despatch Company, set up in 1859 to build an underground railway for use by the Post Office. It was a time when horse-drawn vehicles cluttered London roads to such an extent that the Post Office saw the need for new and faster ways to transport letters and parcels to its eight sorting offices in London. The answer was to build its own underground railway network specifically for the purpose. Spurred on by the success enjoyed by trials elsewhere in London, thoughts turned to the use of a pneumatic railway to transport letters and parcels quickly, cleanly and cost-effectively. The London Pneumatic Despatch Company began laying pneumatic tubes under the streets of London and, in 1863, as the first line opened to run from Euston Station, *The Times* newspaper reported:

> Between the pneumatic despatch and the subterranean railways, the days ought to be fast approaching when the ponderous goods vans which now fly between station and station shall disappear for ever from the streets of London.

The pneumatic railway system carried on transporting mail until 1874, when the Post Office cancelled the contract because the use of the railway was no longer economically viable. The London Pneumatic Despatch Company closed the following year. When the Post Office underground railway was resurrected in 1913, the system was built to use electric trains. Construction was halted during the First World War and so it was 1927 before the new railway opened. It ran until as late as 2003. The tunnels still exist and in later years became a popular tourist attraction.

The Crystal Palace pneumatic railway

The Crystal Palace was the world's largest glass structure. It was built in London's Hyde Park and completed in 1851 to house The Great Exhibition, designed to display the works of industry from around the world. The exhibition opened in May that year and closed in October, after which the Crystal Palace was carefully dismantled, transported piece by piece across London and rebuilt as the centre point of a kind of Victorian theme park which opened to the public in 1854. Outside attractions included tidal lakes with rocks and rapids, the country's largest maze, an area devoted to the study of geology and a kind of forerunner of today's roller coasters called the Topsy-Turvy Railway. By 1864, the attractions also included the first passenger-carrying pneumatic railway.

The railway was the brainchild of civil engineer Thomas Rammell. It was built in a 600-yard brick tunnel 10 feet high and 9 feet wide between the two main

Entrance to the pneumatic railway that ran for a few brief months at the Crystal Palace in south London.

gates to the park, and housed a carriage carrying thirty-five passengers. The air needed to move the carriage came from a steam-driven 22-foot fan at one end. To maintain the airtight seal necessary to cause the carriage to move along the tunnel, it was surrounded by a fringe of bristles that brushed the walls. Passengers entered the carriage through iron doors. Once closed, the fan was started and its air blew through vents in the tunnel floor to propel the carriage along railway tracks. For return trips, the fan was reversed to set up a vacuum that caused the carriage to move back in the opposite direction by extracting air through grills in the tunnel roof. The railway operated for only two months, during which time, passengers were charged 6d (2½p) for each trip.

Waterloo to Whitehall

The short life of the Crystal Palace pneumatic railway did nothing to deter an even more ambitious project that was suggested next: a tunnel under the river Thames to take passengers from Waterloo on the south bank to Whitehall on the north bank.

The plan was to build two underground stations, one at each end of the route. These would then be joined by a tunnel made from an iron tube encased in concrete, supported on brick piers anchored into the riverbed. A 22-foot fan situated at the Waterloo side would be used to propel the carriage by blowing it to Whitehall, then sucking it back again to Waterloo. Iron doors across the tracks at each end of the line would prevent air being blown into the stations. The carriages would have first and second class compartments.

Such a project would of course be costly, so investors were sought, assuring them of a good return on investments. If carriages were run every few minutes, charging fares of 2d (just under 1p) for first class travellers and half that for second class, and if the carriages ran from 7.00 am to midnight, then £23,268 would be raised per year. Investors took the bait and work began in 1865. A year later, the collapse of wholesale discount bank Overend, Gurney and Company in London, coupled with the abandonment of the silver standard in Italy, led to a banking crisis. Funding for the railway dried up, pleas for new funds fell on deaf ears and the project was eventually abandoned in 1869.

From South Kensington station to the Albert Hall

The story of the pneumatic railway was typically one in which great things were promised in advance, but with little success to follow. In 1877, Thomas Rammell, by no means disheartened by the short life of his Crystal Palace railway, tried again with a much more ambitious project. His plan this time was to build a pneumatic railway to provide passengers who alighted at South Kensington Underground station with a simple and comfortable way of accessing the various attractions of the area. With one terminus at the station and the other close to the Royal Albert Hall, visitors would then have a convenient link to the concert hall, as well as museums and horticultural gardens. The *Illustrated London News* showed a careful enthusiasm for the project. In June 1877, the periodical stated:

> No doubt our readers will be familiar with the pneumatic system in which passengers are blown through a tube by a gentle gale of two or three ounces of pressure to the square inch in well-lighted, comfortable carriages free from smoke, dust, heat and smell.

It went on to describe the various failures of the system in the past, but added:

> As far as we can ascertain after careful inquiry and investigation of the system, the failures have had nothing whatever to do with the mechanical principles involved. There is no doubt that Mr Rammell can blow a train loaded with passengers through a tube, say, a mile long, with ease, certainty and economy, while the passengers will travel with a comfort as regards ventilation, quite unknown on the steam worked underground railway.

Rammell got together a board of directors for his company, which was supported by the Metropolitan and District railway companies, and a 4½ per cent dividend was guaranteed for investors in the scheme, which required £60,000 capital. Plans began to be drawn up.

The tunnel was to be made of brick with a paved floor, rising from South Kensington Underground station and travelling uphill to the Royal Albert Hall

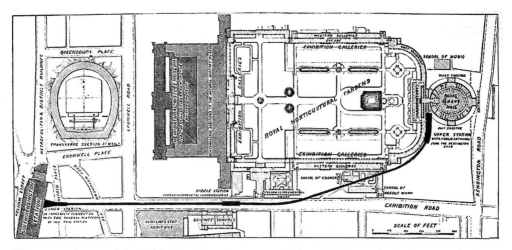

The proposed route of the South Kensington Pneumatic Railway that was never built.

with a gradient of 1:48. This time the train would be blown along it, not by a fan as had been the case in previous pneumatic railways, but by a huge centrifugal pump driven by two steam engines. The train was planned to consist of six carriages, travelling on rails with a 4-foot gauge, and capable of carrying 200 passengers. When the train was not running, it was suggested that the tunnel would be open to the public to walk its length. The *Illustrated London News* waxed lyrical about the plans: 'No novelty is involved in the scheme and of its mechanical success we have no doubt.'

But despite elaborate plans and the enthusiasm of the press and engineers alike, the proposed railway was never built. Thomas Rammell died in 1879 after developing diabetes.

Outside London

Although the majority of plans for pneumatic railways were centred on London, there were some plans for systems in other areas of the country, as well as overseas.

One such scheme was planned to travel under the river Mersey, connecting Liverpool and Birkenhead. The tunnel was built, but then plans were changed for it to be used by steam locomotives.

Plans for a tunnel under the English Channel connecting Britain to France were considered as early as 1802, and one very serious proposal was presented to the Exposition Universelle of Paris in 1867. Neither came to fruition, but in 1869 tentative unfulfilled plans were formulated for a Channel tunnel that utilised a pneumatic railway. That too foundered. It wasn't until 1875 that the idea of a tunnel under the Channel began to seem like a reality, by which time the pneumatic railway idea had been abandoned. Serious work on the tunnel, however, did begin, only to be eventually cancelled in 1898. In the end, it was close to another 100 years, in 1994, before the dream of a tunnel connecting the two countries was successfully realised.

Atmospheric railways

Most pneumatic railways worked by blowing or sucking a carriage along an enclosed tube. But there was another type, more often known as an atmospheric railway, which brought the train and its carriages out into the open. The motive power was once again air pressure, but this time in the form of a vacuum produced inside a pipe laid between a railway line's twin tracks and used to drive a piston attached to the train above. Pumping engines placed in large brick-built buildings at regular intervals along the line produced the necessary vacuum in the pipe. The 'engine'

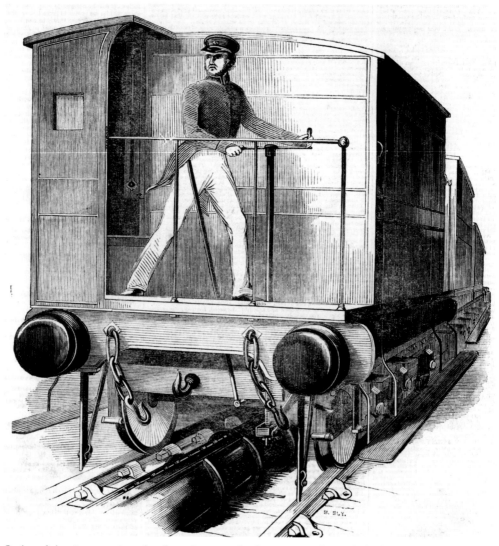

On board the piston carriage that drew the train, the driver screws down the brake, while a gauge on the wall to his right displays the air pressure.

that pulled the carriages was nothing like the traditional concept, not least because it required no actual means of locomotion itself, only an attachment to the piston below. It usually consisted of a carriage similar to those being towed, but with an open platform at the front where the driver stood. To operate the train he needed only a reference to the air pressure being applied and a brake.

The idea became very popular very fast – and then declined in popularity at much the same rate. Between 1844 and 1860 four atmospheric railways were built: in England between Exeter and Newton Abbot, and between London and Croydon; in Ireland between Kingstown and Dalkey; and in France along the St Germain

Starcross pumping station, which still stands beside the railway lines in South Devon.

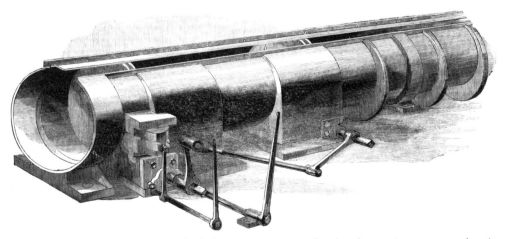

The pipe of a pneumatic railway in which the vacuum was introduced to drive a piston connected to the railway above.

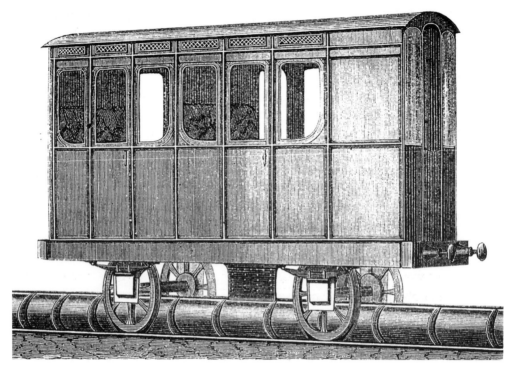

Atmospheric railway carriage on the St Germain line in France.

line outside Paris. In 1854, when Joseph Paxton, designer of the Crystal Palace, formulated designs to build a glass structure called The Great Victorian Way to encircle the centre of London, he planned to have an atmospheric railway running around its perimeter. His plans never came to fruition.

For proponents of atmospheric railways, however, the scheme seemed like the future. The loss of power that came from conventional locomotives having to pull their own weight was avoided. Trains could not travel in opposite directions on the same length of track, avoiding potential accidents. If one train stopped through loss of power, all the trains on the line stopped for the same reason, again avoiding possible collisions. They were safer too because the lack of a fire to heat boilers and generate steam meant the chances of stray sparks setting wooden coaches or luggage alight were eradicated. Calculations also showed that the cost per mile of running an atmospheric railway was something like £15,120, compared to a steam system costing more like £37,600 per mile per annum. Yet despite these and many other positive considerations, atmospheric railways failed.

One of the greatest problems was maintaining a suitable seal between the piston in the pipe and its connection to the railway outside via a slit in said pipe. The usual method was to introduce a series of hinged leather flaps along the length of the slit. As the train passed over, each flap lifted ahead of the piston and dropped back after it passed.

The rise and fall of the Exeter to Newton Abbot atmospheric railway is an example of the system's initial success and subsequent failure. When the 20-mile stretch of line opened in 1846, steam locomotives were at first used, but by 1847 an atmospheric infrastructure had been built, put in place and tested. At the start of 1848, atmospheric trains began to run, achieving speeds of up to 70 miles per hour and operating to a strict timetable.

Not long after the inauguration of the atmospheric system, however, problems began to be apparent. Rain and sea air led to the leather flaps becoming quickly degraded, which led to a loss of air pressure. A second problem was rats, who were prone to eat the tallow used to keep the leather supple, again resulting in a loss of air pressure. As the planned timetable began to prove unreliable, and the pumping engines were forced to work harder to maintain the air pressure, costs rocketed. It was decided that it would prove too costly to replace the seals, with no guarantee that the replacements would not degrade as fast as the originals. By the end of 1848, South Devon's atmospheric railway had closed and steam locomotives had been reinstated.

When atmospheric railways worked, they worked well. They were economic, clean and silent. But in the end they were defeated by the inherent problems associated with their methods of operation, as well as new and rapid advances in steam-powered locomotion.

A pneumatic train at Dawlish, heading towards Exeter.

The Pioneering Journeys of *Daddy Long-Legs*

Imagine a means of transport that looks like a traditional railway carriage mounted at the centre of the deck of a huge yacht. Now consider that strange combination mounted at the top of four 24-foot stilt-like legs with flanged wheels at each of their bases running along railway tracks. Then think of how it might be if those tracks were running, not across the land, but under the sea, with the carriage full of passengers riding high above the waves. It sounds like something out of an imaginary steampunk world but, from 1896 until 1901, this strange method of transport existed and operated along the south coast of England. It's inventor was Magnus Volk, who called it his Seaside Electric Railway, giving the single

Daddy Long-Legs, running through the water at high tide.

carriage on stilts the name *Pioneer*. Because of its shape and design, the public soon nicknamed it *Daddy Long-Legs*.

Volk was the son of a German immigrant clockmaker who settled in Brighton. From an early age Volk Junior was fascinated by electricity and model making. He was the first person in Brighton to own a telephone and to equip his house with electric light. Appointed as electrical engineer to the Corporation of Brighton in 1883, he soon installed electricity in the Brighton Pavilion, the town's one-time royal residence. He also built a very early type of electric car and, in 1883, went on to open Britain's first electric railway, which ran along the coast at Brighton. Its successor still runs there today.

In 1890, Volk looked into the possibility of extending his electric railway east to the town of Rottingdean. He immediately ran into an obstacle in the shape of high cliffs that stood in the way of his proposed line. The cliffs were too steep for a railway engine to climb and the undercliff was not stable enough to support the tracks required for a conventional railway. So he turned attention away from the cliffs and proposed a daring scheme to lay the tracks along the shore, exposed at low tide and under water at high tide.

Building the railway

The carriage was built by the Gloucester Railway Carriage and Wagon Company, which set up business at Gloucester in 1860 to make railway products that included goods wagons, passenger coaches and stock for the London Underground railway. The carriage built for Volk consisted of a veranda 45 feet long and 22 feet wide surrounding an enclosed saloon, something like a traditional railway carriage inside but with an open promenade deck on its roof. The saloon was equipped with plush, upholstered seats, curtains and even plants. A maximum of 160 passengers could be accommodated.

To run *Pioneer*, 25-horsepower electric motors drove long shafts which ran inside the four tubular legs and were geared to the wheels at each base, which were enclosed in metal casings, shaped to push debris out of their path as it made its way through the sea. The electric current to drive the motors was picked up from two connecting rods tipped with small wheels, designed to run along overhead cables slung between pylons beside the track. The required electricity was generated by a gas-driven generator, producing 500 volts and housed below a pier at Rottingdean. The wheels on the two legs on one side of the carriage ran on one set of tracks, and the wheels on the two legs on the other side ran on a second set of tracks.

Building the tracks to run *Pioneer* involved extremely hard labour during 1894's winter, which proved to be cold enough to freeze the sea on the beach. Naturally,

Pioneer running dry at low tide.

the labourers could work only at low tide, retiring when the sea came in to cover their work and returning as it receded. In these difficult and freezing conditions, they first dug square holes along the route which were filled with concrete, partly buried but with chunks standing above ground. The tracks were fastened to the concrete blocks. In this way, the four rails required for *Pioneer's* operation were laid, consisting of two parallel sets of two-rail tracks. The route was kept as level as possible, its steepest gradient no more than 1:300.

Running the railway

Pioneer's first outing rook place on 28 November 1896. Passengers alighted via a pier running from the beach's promenade, level with the deck of the carriage. Present on that first journey were the Mayor of Brighton, the Chairman of Rottingdean Parish Council, the town's two members of parliament and other dignitaries. They were transported on a journey that took thirty-five minutes to cover 2¾ miles from Brighton to Rottingdean. On its return, a celebratory luncheon was held. After that, *Pioneer* was thrown open to the public for the price of sixpence (2½p) a trip.

For the first week of operation, everything went well. The railway was rarely short of passengers eager to experience the ride, even though high tides and the effort of propelling the carriage through deep water often led to a breakdown midway,

Passengers boarding the carriage at Kemptown in Brighton.

How a voyage on *Daddy Long-Legs* was advertised on posters of the time.

with *Pioneer* coming to a halt for several hours just at the point where a ventilation shaft for Brighton's main sewer emerged into the open air. Nevertheless, the press reports were enthusiastic, with pundits who prophesised that Volk's invention was set to revolutionise sea travel.

A week after the official opening tragedy struck during one of the worst storms ever remembered on this part of the south coast. *Pioneer*, lashed to its moorings at Rottingdean Pier, broke free, overturned and was smashed apart by the strong winds. Some of the rails and poles that held the overhead cables were also damaged. Magnus Volk, however, was undeterred. He raised cash, salvaged *Pioneer* and had it up and running by the following July. For the next few years it carried thousands of passengers, including the then Prince of Wales, who made the trip twice on 20 February 1898.

The end of *Pioneer*

The year 1900 spelt the beginning of the end for Volk's Seaside Electric Railway. Following the summer season, when it had to be closed for repair, the local council announced that sea defence work meant the *Pioneer*'s rails would have to be moved further out to sea. It was an impractical idea. Moving the rails into the deeper water would have meant an extra strain on the electric motors that drove the carriage, which already often had difficulty moving much faster than walking pace when the tide was particularly high, and it wasn't practical to replace the electric motors with more powerful versions. On top of that there was the impracticality, not to say impossibility, of laying tracks actually under the water, as opposed to laying them on the shore when the tide was out. In 1901, council workmen moved in to remove sections of the tracks to carry out the projected work on sea defences. *Pioneer* was

Pioneer left to rot on the beach at Rottingdean, later to be broken up for scrap.

All that remains today: stone blocks at Rottingdean, part of the foundations on which the tracks were laid.

taken to Rottingdean Pier, where it remained for the next nine years, slowly rotting away, until it was broken up for scrap in 1910. The pier survived for about another four years, before also being demolished.

Today, when the tide is out, a few rows of jagged concrete blocks can still be seen straggling along the shoreline between Brighton and Rottingdean. They are all that remain of the foundations on which the tracks were laid and on which *Pioneer*, also known as *Daddy Long-Legs*, ran for five glorious years.

Impossible Journeys

There were times in the history of rail travel when newspaper reporters allowed their imaginations to run away with them. When Magnus Volk's Seaside Electric Railway was announced there were those who envisioned a day when similar undersea railways would run from Dover to Calais, or even London to New York. None of the reports, however, seemed to have considered how the tracks might be laid under the English Channel, let alone the Atlantic Ocean. Inventors and designers too sometimes came up with plans for railway lines that were totally impractical. Here are two preposterous ideas that, for reasons obvious to anyone who gave a thought to the feasibilities, never came to fruition.

London to New York Railway

Of all the weird and wonderful schemes dreamed of for routes by rail, surely one of the most ambitious – not to say unworkable – was the idea that a railway might be built all the way from London to New York. The plan was not, as might be suspected, to tunnel under the Atlantic Ocean or even to build a bridge across it, but to take the long way round, over and under land, leaving England and travelling across France, Austria, Poland, Russia, Alaska, Canada and finally, America. The journey, which would take place without the need for passengers to once change trains, would take twelve days to travel a total of 14,317 miles.

In all of this distance only two stretches of water stood in the way: 30 miles under the English Channel connecting England and France, and another 38 miles under the Bering Strait, connecting Siberia and Alaska.

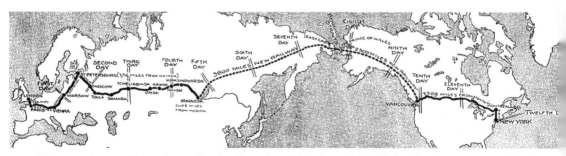

The route that would have been taken by the proposed London to New York railway.

There was nothing new about the idea of tunnelling under these two stretches of water. Plans for a tunnel under the English Channel date back as far as 1802. Then, with the rise in popularity of steam railways in Britain, another proposal was suggested in the 1830s. In 1855, Queen Victoria, along with Napoleon III of France, approved a plan for a tunnel. In 1877, shafts were dug at Sangatte in France and St Margaret's Bay in England, but were abandoned due to flooding. In 1880, a new shaft was sunk between Folkestone and Dover and serious tunnelling began, only to be abandoned in 1898 after a series of technical problems and political setbacks.

Likewise, in Russia, proposals to build a tunnel under the sea from Siberia to Alaska were considered in the 1870s, and in 1886, a geological survey was presented to the United States Senate. There had even been thoughts of bridging the Bering Strait, using the Diomede Islands, situated along the proposed route. These plans had been superseded, however, due to advances made in tunnelling technology of the time. Not only the American Senate but also the Russian Court expressed an interest in the idea of a tunnel between the two countries.

So, by the time the ambitious London to New York railway scheme was announced, the two sea crossings involved would not have been seen as major obstacles. Here's the route that was suggested:

London to Paris (via a tunnel under the English Channel): 230 miles.
Paris to Vienna: 625 miles.
Vienna to Warsaw: 350 miles.
Warsaw to St Petersburg: 650 miles.
St Petersburg to Moscow: 400 miles.
Moscow to Irkutsk: 3,405 miles.
Irkutsk to East Cape: 3,800 miles.
East Cape to Cape Prince of Wales (via a tunnel under the Bering Strait): 38 miles.
Cape Prince of Wales to Vancouver: 2,300 miles.
Vancouver to Montreal: 2,209 miles.
Montreal to New York: 310 miles.

Much of this network was already in place. As well as the two tunnels, two new lines would have needed to have been built. The first was from Irkutsk to East Cape and, once the Bering Strait had been tunnelled, from Cape Prince of Wales to Vancouver.

All of this was enthusiastically reported in a 1906 issue of *Popular Mechanics* magazine. Needless to say, the London to New York railway never happened, even though the dream lived on. The 1960s saw a proposal for a tunnel under the Atlantic that would be travelled by vactrains, which work by magnetic levitation in a tunnel from which the air has been removed to a near vacuum to reduce resistance and allowing speeds of up to 5,000 miles per hour. More interestingly, in 2015 Russia unveiled plans for a high-speed rail and road network, called the Trans-Eurasian Belt Development, from Eastern Europe, across Siberia, over the Bering Strait to Alaska, which, when extended at each end, would make rail and road travel possible between London and New York, following a route significantly close to the early 1900s plan of linking the two capitals.

A journey to the centre of the earth

If a plan to run a railway from London to New York seems improbable, then the idea of a railway running from the surface straight down a huge shaft to terminate at the centre of the earth must be little short of preposterous. Yet, that's exactly what was proposed and reported in the engineering press of 1913.

The man behind the scheme was French scientist and author Camille Flammarion, who saw an opportunity of employing the armies of Europe to dig a shaft and tap the sources of heat and power stored beneath the surface of the earth. Such sources, it was determined, would be of immense value to mankind. Not only that, but there was also the prospect of finding huge supplies of gold and diamonds buried in the earth as it was dug out.

Having put the idea forward, Flammarion was the first to admit that, in the then current state of engineering science, harnessing the forces present at the centre of the earth would result in the destruction of any apparatus used for the purpose. That said, Flammarion was confident that, within a generation, science would find ways to overcome such difficulties and the day would dawn when a journey to the centre of the earth would be no more difficult than boarding and travelling on a normal railway. And so he pressed on with his description of how the scheme might be developed.

How a journey to the centre of the earth might have been undertaken by train.

One obstacle he foresaw was hauling the debris dug out of the shaft up to the surface. The problem was that steel cables of the length required for the job would break under their own weight. A system of elevators, each travelling on cables for separate sections of the shaft, was considered and abandoned, mainly because they wouldn't be fast enough, especially when loads being transported needed to be transferred from lower elevators to higher ones along the route. And so, according to Flammarion, only one form of transport would be practical: a spiral railway running around and down the inside edge of the shaft.

Two tracks would be needed, one for downward traffic and the other for upward traffic. A radius of at least 500 feet would be required for the scheme to work, which meant the shaft would need to be 1,000 feet wide. In its centre there would be a conduit with a diameter of 500 feet to force air down to the lower depths for purposes of ventilation, not to mention the necessity of the workmen having to breathe.

Another aspect anticipated by Flammarion was that gravity lessened the lower the shaft sank, making work and transportation easier. The weakened gravity at greater depths also meant the chances of workmen falling and being killed were decreased. Eventually, at the centre of the earth they would have no weight at all. By the same token, the weight of the railway engines and their rolling stock would appear to lose weight so that it might become difficult to keep them on the tracks. But Flammarion had the answer to that. It would, he said, simply be a matter of substituting some new force, such as magnetism, to take the place of gravity and so keep train wheels on tracks.

These trains would be driven by electricity. With an incline of 1:4 it was estimated that a journey from the surface to the centre of the earth, travelling at 40 miles per hour, would take about a month for the descent and, with the necessity of travelling slower on the return, about two months to come up again.

If science of the future permitted such journeys, Flammarion visualised what it would be like for the train travellers, making the journey as tourists. There would be no night or day, so these conditions might have to be induced artificially by electric lighting. As the train drew deeper into the ground the passengers would experience a lightness of their bodies, growing more pronounced with the increased depth. At a depth of, say, 2,000 miles, there would be a need for the passengers to wear metallic suits. Arrival at the centre, and with no gravity, the passengers would be able to swim in the air, or walk naturally with the aid of magnetism on an electrically charged surface.

Flammarion admitted, however, that it wasn't likely that the train passengers would care to stay too long at the centre of the earth. A few days, or weeks at the most, would be sufficient before the passengers boarded the train for the two-month journey back to sun and sky.

New York's Lost Railways

At the end of the nineteenth century New York City was gridlocked with horse traffic. Travel from one spot to another across the metropolis was uncomfortable at best, made unbearable during rush hours, when an estimated 500,000 people were transported around and across the city every twenty-four hours. The sheer volume of traffic meant progress on the roads was slow, with bad weather inhibiting movement even more and leading to unpredictable behaviour in horses drawing passenger vehicles that were too hot in summer, too cold in winter and overcrowded all of the time. The railways didn't fare much better, being as crowded and uncomfortable as the horse-drawn vehicles on the roads.

In 1869, in an early attempt at alleviating the problem, inventor, publisher and patent lawyer Alfred Beach began building a pneumatic railway under Broadway in New York City. His Beach Pneumatic Transit Company succeeded in building a tunnel 312 feet long in just fifty-eight days. Beach initially put the scheme forward

Albert Beach's experimental pneumatic railway under Broadway.

as a system for transporting mail, but by the time it was completed he had opened it to passengers with the idea of extending the line to Central Park. At the time of its opening, however, there was no real final destination for the railway, and so passengers could only ride through the tunnel to the end of the line and back again, for no reason other than the actual experience. Nevertheless, interest was high at the start, but delays in getting permission to extend the line to anywhere worth visiting, coinciding with a stock market crash that halted any potential investment, meant that public interest eventually waned and the railway was closed in 1873.

A few years before Beach endeavoured to get his pneumatic railway accepted, other more ambitious plans had already been formulated to solve the congestion problem. They included a railway 30 feet below the road, an elevated railway running on a viaduct above the road and, between them, a moving footway to speed up pedestrian traffic.

The Arcade Railway

The proposed Arcade Railway.

At the heart of this plan was another railway whose tracks were to run beneath Broadway, with branches at 23rd Street travelling east and west. This railway was planned to serve not just stations that would lead to the surface at each corner of Broadway, but also whole streets of underground shops, built with their frontages opening into what had previously been the basements of as many as 1,700 of the original stores 30 feet above. The plan was originated by entrepreneurs H.C. Gardner and Melville C. Smith, who presented their proposal in 1866 for what they called the Arcade Railway.

Their proposal was to build an artificial road on the level of the original street. This would be supported on hollow iron pillars, which would also act as drains. Below this, 30 feet under the road, wide footpaths were to be built each side of an arcade with the underground shops lining each side. Between the footpaths, railway tracks would be built. The railway carriages were at first envisaged to be drawn by horses, but later a pneumatic railway system was proposed with four tracks, two for passengers and two for freight. The tunnel would be lit by gas, but in the roof over the footway and railway tracks, glass panels would let in as much light as possible from above during daylight hours.

In this way, it would add a whole new storey to Broadway, one of the most well-known streets in New York, the walking capacity of the area would be doubled and the passenger-carrying facilities would be quadrupled.

The cost of this audacious plan was estimated at $20 million, which could be raised by increasing the rents of the stores that now had a new storey to attract customers. Between 1870 and 1889, plans were presented to the legislature five times, and each time they were turned down, finally defeated by objections from property owners along the length of Broadway.

How the pneumatic railway intended to run under Broadway might have looked.

The Railway Sidewalk

New York in the 1870s also saw a proposal from inventor and businessman Alfred Speer for a moving pedestrian road, dubbed the Railway Sidewalk or Endless Traveling. His idea would place this moving belt, the width of a normal pedestrian path, on an elevated platform supported by 14-foot high iron pillars on a looped route up and down Broadway and accessed by ornamental stairways at street corners. Moving at about 10 miles per hour, it would aid pedestrians by boosting the normal walking speed of approximately 4 miles per hour to something more like 14 miles per hour. Travellers who did not wish to walk could also sit in cabins

The proposed Railway Sidewalk for pedestrians, complete with moving benches, shelters and ladies' drawing rooms.

like small railway carriages or on benches, both of which were carried along on the moving path. The cost would be five cents a ride.

The conveyor belt that was at the heart of the moving path was to be between 16 feet and 18 feet wide and positioned 12 feet from the nearest buildings. It was to be operated by underground steam engines one mile apart driving belts via the iron pillars to the moving pathway that transported walkers or riders. Shelters, which included special drawing rooms for ladies, would be placed at regular intervals along the route for people who wanted to take refuge from bad weather, or who wished to take advantage of toilet facilities, smoking and reading rooms.

In 1872, the estimated cost was quoted at $3,772,500. Reaction from the public was, to some extent, derisory. Even so, state legislature initially approved Speer's plans in 1873 and 1874. Despite that, the scheme was eventually vetoed because of the way it might interfere with the more conventional pedestrian thoroughfares, as well as its cost and objections to its proposed route.

Elevated railways

Elevated railways in which trains run on a series of viaducts above roads were once common in New York in the mid-to-late nineteenth century. It was an era that began in 1866 with the inspiration of self-trained civil engineer Charles Harvey,

Charles Harvey takes a test run on his elevated railway.

who was granted a charter for work to begin on the Greenwich Street Elevated Railway. The plan was for carriages to be drawn along a track supported by a single row of columns, using a chain that ran between the rails on an endless loop driven by a stationary engine. The line opened in 1868 but, despite the carriages being more luxurious than their earthbound counterparts, passengers were few, and the railway was closed in 1870. A half-hearted attempt to resurrect the line the following year also failed and the railway's properties were finally sold at auction in 1872.

A different, more ambitious and ultimately more successful scheme came from inventor Rufus Gilbert. Working as an assistant superintendent for the New Jersey Central Railroad, he came up with a plan for an elevated railway for which he was granted a patent in 1870. As with other elevated railways, Gilbert's design was for railway carriages that ran on elevated pillars in the form of decorative elevated arches above the road. Unlike other designs, the carriages did not run on conventional tracks. In their place the arched pillars above the road supported tubes, to facilitate a pneumatic railway, with the carriages blown along the tubes by compressed air.

By the time building began in 1874, the pneumatic railway had been abandoned in favour of the more conventional tracks, now supported on less decorative arches and used to run normal steam trains, with stations placed at regular intervals along

How a proposed elevated railway in New York's Ninth Avenue might have looked.

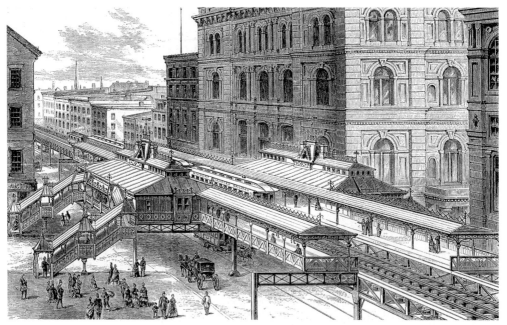

A station on Gilbert's elevated railway at the corner of Twenty-Third Street and Sixth Avenue.

A station waiting room
on Gilbert's elevated
railway.

the route. In the years ahead, Gilbert was given permission to extend his railway and by 1878, when it opened, the Gilbert Elevated Railway had become a major landmark in the city, attracting millions of passengers.

Soon after the railway opened, however, Gilbert was swindled and forced out of the company by his partners, leaving him impoverished. He died in 1885, aged 53.

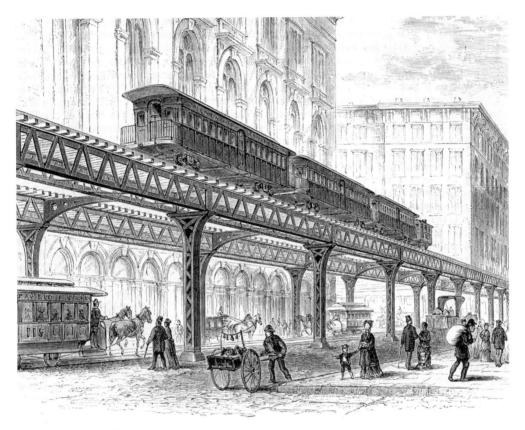

Elevated railway at Third Avenue.

For a few brief years, elevated railways continued to operate in New York. But in the end, they were considered slow and dirty, eventually to be superseded by the cleaner and more efficient underground networks of the New York Subway. Even though some parts of today's subway still emerge from underground to run on elevated lines in the outer boroughs, elevated railways in New York are now a largely forgotten part of the city's past.

The New York City Bowery Elevated Railway.

Pedal Power, Horse Power, Railcars and More

First there was steam, later there was electricity; in between there was air power. These were some of the popular, as well as less common, ways by which passengers were conveyed along railway lines. But they were by no means the only means of propulsion. Over the years, pedal-powered cycles, motor vehicles and even horses took to the tracks to provide novel, but rarely long-lasting, methods of rail transport. And along the way, there were a few fanciful ideas that never got past the drawing boards of dreamers.

Horse-powered engines

As early as 1829, Americans saw the value of using horses to draw carts along railway tracks in much the same way they might have pulled wagons along roads. Running a cart on rails gave a smoother, more energy-effective journey than dragging one over rough roads, which meant horses were not required to work as hard. Before steam was introduced to the line, the Baltimore and Ohio Railroad was among those that saw the advantages, claiming that a single horse could pull freight along a railway line equal to the same weight pulled by twelve horses on a road at speeds of up to 15 miles per hour.

Horse-drawn rail cart on the Baltimore and Ohio Railroad.

The amazing Italian Impulsoria horse-driven engine.

A more spectacular use of horse power, however, arrived in the UK in 1850 when the London & South Western Railway introduced a new type of locomotive driven, rather than drawn, by teams of horses. This strange device was called the Impulsoria.

Looking like no other form of railway engine, the Impulsoria was the brainchild of Clemente Masserano, an Italian inventor. The machine was built in Italy and brought to England, where it was installed at the Nine Elms rail terminus in south-west London. It took the form of an open-topped carriage whose inclined floor consisted of a kind of treadmill. Either two or four horses were led into the carriage, where they were tethered. As they walked, they remained in place, while the treadmill moved backwards under their hooves. This caused an axle to turn, which rotated a pulley connected by a rope to the vehicle's driving wheels. Different diameters of pulley acted like gears to allow varying travelling speeds, while the horses maintained the same pace. In this way, any speed from normal walking pace up to an ambitiously estimated 60 miles per hour was claimed to be possible. Early experiments showed that the horse-driven locomotive was capable of pulling thirty wagons up an incline at 7 miles per hour. According to the way the gears were set, the vehicle could run forwards or backwards without having to change the direction the horses faced, while a free wheel arrangement meant Impulsoria could continue moving when the horses stopped walking, or the horses could walk with the machine standing still.

With the horses working for eight hours – considered the norm for a working horse at that time – Impulsoria could cover eight journeys, each of 30 miles in a day.

With four horses costing about two shillings (10p) each per day to feed, the outlay for a day's running amounted to no more than eight shillings (40p), as opposed to £6, which was the equivalent cost of running a steam locomotive over the same distance. In this way, locomotive power could be cheaply introduced to hitherto unapproachable branch lines otherwise considered too expensive to operate.

The initial tests were a success and Impulsoria was shown at The Great Exhibition in 1851. Even so, railway companies failed to place orders and horse-driven locomotives never truly materialised as serious rivals to steam.

The rise of the railcars

Given that pneumatic rubber tyres were so popular on road vehicles, it isn't too surprising that, for a while at least in the 1930s, they seemed to be the way forward for railways as well. Several innovators came up with the idea, but it was French tyre manufacturer André Michelin who first took it seriously. His reasoning was that using rubber would give a smoother, quieter ride and also provide better traction than more conventional metal wheels on metal tracks, accelerating faster and allowing later braking than metal-wheeled trains. Michelin trialled rubber tyres on a vehicle he called La Micheline, but this and similar vehicles that followed became known more generically as railcars. They didn't look at all like the traditional idea of railway engines, but more like motor coaches on rails.

Like their metal counterparts, railcar tyres used metal flanges to keep the wheels on the tracks. The tyres were inflated to a pressure of 85 pounds per square

La Micheline under test in France.

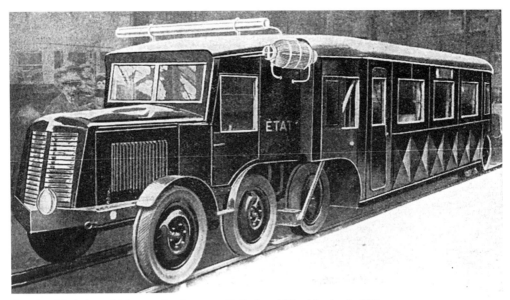

Another Michelin vehicle, running between Oxford and Bletchley in the UK.

inch, but incorporated internal wooden hoops so that any puncture in the rubber would cause the tyre to deflate only a little, thus avoiding derailment. In such circumstances, it was reckoned that a wheel could be changed in five minutes. In 1931, tests were conducted in France, where La Micheline travelled 66.5 miles from Paris to Deauville in two hours and three minutes. By 1935, fourteen thirty-six-seater Michelin railcars had travelled more than 800,000 miles on French railways.

Around this time, the concept was brought to the UK, where it was trialled on the London, Midland & Scottish Railway, otherwise known as the LMS line, between Oxford and Bletchley. The railcar under test used a 27-horsepower petrol engine that could be driven in forward or reverse at similar speeds via a four-speed gearbox. The engine drove four wheels at the front of the railcar, while further wheels at the rear acted as load bearers. Brakes were operated in a similar way to a road vehicle, and of course no steering was needed, since the vehicle's direction was guided by the rails on which it ran. It could therefore be driven by anyone with experience of bus or coach operation. Although *Commercial Motor* magazine of 16 February 1932 enthusiastically reported the trialled railcar as travelling at 92 miles per hour, it is more likely that it attained speeds of no more than 60 miles per hour. Its acceleration to these speeds was fast compared to that of a steam engine, reaching 50 miles per hour in 1,000 yards. The early railcars were solid bodied from the front to the rear. Later versions were designed with the front half consisting of a lorry-like cab with a petrol engine under its bonnet, and a rear half that resembled much more a traditional railway carriage.

The rather more streamlined Coventry railcar.

The driver's seat of a Coventry railcar.

Railcars were also built in Britain with the assistance of motor manufacturer Armstrong Siddeley in Coventry, after which town they were named. A Coventry railcar was much more streamlined than the early Michelin railcars, looking less like a huge motor coach and more like a long pullman car type railway carriage. It incorporated double seats for fifty-six passengers, safety glass in extra-wide windows, a luggage compartment, and was lit and heated by electricity. The driver sat on a sprung padded seat in a kind of submarine-like conning tower that protruded from the roof, giving him a 360-degree view of everything around him. The railcars were fitted with 240-horsepower engines and self-changing gearboxes that attained speeds of 70 miles per hour in forward and reverse.

Other rather more half-hearted attempts were made at building railcars in America, where it was thought they might service outlying, less populated areas of the country.

They had no long-lasting successes. One of the major problems was that railcars required so many more wheels than a traditional railway carriage, and that the rubber wore out fast compared to the nearly indestructible metal wheels. In the end, the railcar, which for a while in the 1930s seemed like a viable proposition, in both Britain and France, was consigned to history.

Velocipedes on rails

The 1800s saw the rise of the velocipede, an early name for what later became the bicycle, tricycle and other forms of pedal-powered transport. They were naturally designed to run on roads. But a few inventors came up with four-wheeled, pedal-powered vehicles to run on normal railway tracks.

An 1881 patent from inventors Omer F. Campbell and Frank L. Prindle show a strange contraption called a railroad velocipede. It was dominated by a large wheel

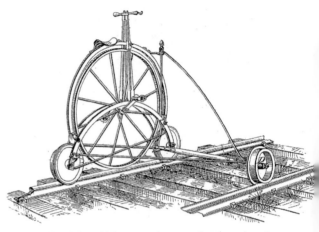

Campbell and Prindle's patent drawing for the railroad velocipede.

with peddles on it and a saddle for the rider, flanked by two smaller wheels front and back, all three of which ran along one railway track. Counterbalancing these three wheels, a fourth was placed at the end of an axle extended to run along the second track. Not long after this, advertisements began to appear for accessories that could be attached to any normal bicycle to allow it to run with its usual two wheels on one railway track and a third attached wheel on the adjacent track. 'No mud, no hills, no dust', the advertisements proclaimed, adding this was the only attachment you have a perfect right to use. It's tempting to wonder how that argument would have stood up against a train coming the other way.

A more logical design, and one that must have been better balanced, appeared in an

An advertisement shows how to convert your normal bicycle for rail use.

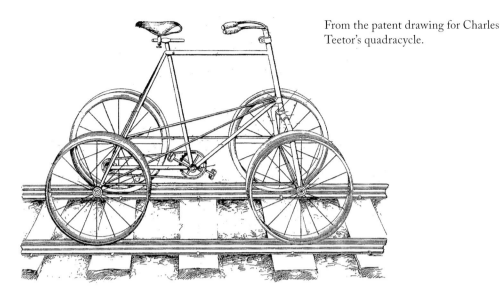

From the patent drawing for Charles Teetor's quadracycle.

1896 patent taken out by Charles Teetor for a quadracycle that he called his railway velocipede. In this, four wheels of equal sizes, two on each side to run on twin railway tracks, supported a framework between them with a saddle, pedals and a chain to drive the back wheels. Handlebars positioned in front of the saddle were obviously there only for the rider to hang on to, since the velocipede could not be steered away from the tracks on which the vehicle ran.

Arthur Hotchkiss's fence-top monorail.

Between these two, in 1892, American inventor Arthur Hotchkiss patented a kind of upside-down bicycle with the wheels on top and the pedals below, running it along a monorail built on the top of a fence between the town of Smithville and Mount Holly, just under 2 miles away. Its purpose was to enable factory workers to travel from the town to their factory in about six minutes. The major design fault was that there was no way for one vehicle to overtake another and, if two were moving in opposite directions, one had to find a siding to move into. Nevertheless, Hotchkiss's bicycle railroad operated for about five years before declining interest forced it to close.

Road-railers

In the 1930s, travelling by road had many advantages over rail, as well as a few disadvantages. Conversely, the opposite was also true. That was the thinking that led transport engineers to begin considering the possibility of designing a new type of vehicle that could be driven along the road to a suitable stretch of railway track, converted in no more than five minutes to running on that track and, on arrival at its destination, converted back again to complete its journey by road. The vehicles became known as road-railers, or sometimes ro-railers.

In one model, special flanged wheels fitted to an ordinary motor car allowed the vehicle to run on railway tracks. The wheels were made of steel. In use, the car's normal tyres were first partially deflated. The steel flanged wheel was then fitted over the tyre, which was then re-inflated to hold it in place. In this way, the flanged wheels ran on the railway track, while the rubber-tyred wheels did the normal job of absorbing shocks and vibrations during the journey.

How metal flanged wheels were fitted over a car's rubber tyres to run on railway tracks.

Such vehicles, it was thought, would be of particular advantage in outlying villages served only by a branch of the main railway line. Not only could the road-railers be utilised for a more convenient method of conveying people and goods, they could also be called into service at certain times of the day or year when roads were more congested than normal.

Above: a road-railer picks up passengers in town. Below: the same road-railer takes on more passengers at a railway station.

The Karrier road-railer, made by English lorry maker Karrier Motors, was a good example of the multi-use vehicle. It was delivered to the London, Midland & Scottish Railway in 1931. Looking a lot like a normal twenty-six-seater coach it complied with both railway and Ministry of Transport regulations. It was fitted with a six-cylinder, 37-horsepower petrol engine, capable of delivering speeds of 60 miles per hour on the road and 75 miles per hour on rails.

Each of the road-railer's axles was fitted with flanged rail wheels, 4 feet 8½ inches apart, compliant with the standard railway gauge. On the outside of these, road wheels with pneumatic tyres were fitted 6 feet 3½ inches apart. For road travel, the two sets of wheels were locked together, since the rail wheels did not touch the ground. At its appointed place of conversion from road to rail, the rails ran within the road, which was made up in the form of a slight incline, the top level with the rail tracks, before tapering off again. The vehicle was driven up the incline and down the other side until the rail wheels were in contact with the tracks. The road wheels, which were on an eccentric drive, were then raised by the driver, freeing them from their lock to the rail wheels and fixing them into position on the vehicle's chassis. To convert the vehicle from rail to road, a similar procedure was carried out in reverse.

Most road-railers were made in the form of coaches, which ran in both England and Holland. The Kaiser Motor Company also made the twin use vehicles in the form of lorries. Like so many transport schemes of the past, road-railers were high among those that must have seemed like a good idea at the time, but failed to survive much beyond their era.

More strange railcars

In the early years of the twentieth century, many different types of vehicle were built or converted to run along railways lines. Here are a few.

- A short stretch of railway line between New Orleans and Mandeville in America supported steam automobiles with railway wheels in place of pneumatic tyres. The coach-type bodies carried twenty-two passengers each.
- A train running in Scotland, consisting of a motive section that resembled a car on rails, pulled a carriage with tiered seating.
- A petrol-driven locomotive once operated as the sole means of transport on a railway line in Kansas. The tracks had originally supported steam locomotives to haul wheat from the fields of the Dakotas to the coast at Galveston. When the steam engines grew too old to operate, they were sold for scrap and the owner realised enough funds to convert a touring car to run along the tracks for a similar purpose.

At St Petersburg in Florida, the problem of finding an inexpensive way to transport ice from docks to a fish warehouse was solved by the use of a handcart equipped with a sail. In an ordinary light wind, it was enough to propel the cart, carrying up to 14,000 pounds of ice, three-quarters of a mile in about three minutes.

Top to bottom: cars on rails running in Scotland, Kansas and New Orleans.

The gyroscope monorail

It was, according to publicity of the time, 'the greatest mechanical sensation in years'. The creation of Irish-born inventor Louis Brennan, what was dubbed 'the railway car of the future' consisted of a carriage whose single set of inline wheels balanced on one rail. In this way it could travel across land and over rivers and ravines at speeds of up to 150 miles per hour. The mechanics behind the invention were based on a child's toy known as a gyroscope.

A gyroscope, the capabilities of which had been known for many years, though often seen as little more than a novelty, incorporated two flywheels that rotated in opposite directions to build up what some saw as a mysterious force of power. When applied to a toy the result was a spinning top, in which the force generated by the flywheels kept the toy upright and stable when placed on any surface, including the tip of a finger or even a length of wire or string along which it could balance and travel. It was known as the top that would not fall over. Applied on a much larger scale to Brennan's monorail car, the result was a carriage that ran on its single rail without overbalancing. With the vehicle supported on pivoted bogies, it was possible for it to travel not only on flat ground, but also around steep curves, on crooked rails and on uneven ground without the danger of derailment. When the land ran out, the rail could be replaced by a strong cable capable of supporting the vehicle over a river or ravine without the danger of it overbalancing. The mechanism could be driven by a petrol engine, oil, gas, steam or electricity.

Great interest was originally shown in the gyroscope monorail, so much so that the British government invested many thousands of pounds to purchase the patent from Brennan and spent thousands more building a 12-foot wide carriage for experimental purposes. The prediction was that once into regular service the cars would be much wider and two or three storeys high.

Although the demonstrations were initially very successful, the monorail car was eventually pronounced as not much more than a highly scientific toy and doubts were expressed about the possibility of the car being blown off the track by high winds. In the end, Brennan's

Louis Brennan's gyroscope monorail.

gyroscope monorail went the way of so many other unconventional means of transport that never quite caught the imagination of the public or of the backers needed to finance them.

Meigs's elevated railway

Josiah Meigs was an American inventor who had an interest in the improvement of public transport. His proposition was for a strangely designed steam-driven monorail that ran on two rails, one above the other. One set of wheels in the base of the engine gripped the upper rail and provided the motive power which moved the train along the track. Lower wheels were in pairs, each at 45 degrees that formed a 'V' shape. These carried the train's weight on the lower rail. The carriages were cylindrical to improve wind resistance. Inside, seats lined each wall and were also positioned along the centre of the tubular carriage.

In using the two rails, one above the other, the monorail could be supported on single pillars, which would take up around a fifth of the space needed by a more traditional elevated railway whose tracks ran side by side. The result was that the streets below would be more open and less shadowed compared to the streets below more traditional elevated railways.

Josiah Meigs's strangely-designed monorail.

In Massachusetts in 1881, Meigs built an experimental track in an attempt to raise investment, and for a while enthusiasm was high. Unfortunately, the scheme ended with the coming of electricity, which Meigs believed could not provide the power needed for his monorail. The opening of a rival elevated railway also contributed to his scheme's downfall. In 1886, Meigs sold the charter rights that he had been granted for the monorail. Failing health from injuries sustained in the American Civil War led to a stroke, from which he died in 1907.

More monorails

Huge torpedo-shaped trains made to run at up to 100 miles per hour while suspended from a single elevated rail were considered by transport authorities in Los Angeles in the 1920s. Built of steel, the cylindrical coaches would have been 60 feet long and capable of seating 100 passengers. The plan was to run them above the streets of crowded cities without materially interfering with the motor traffic below. The single rail would have been supported on narrow structures with twin carriages suspended on each side. If the plans had been accepted and the unusual method of transport built and put into action, it was claimed that travel times and costs could be significantly reduced.

Another more traditional type of monorail promised the thrills of air travel with the passenger capacity of a train in a 150-miles-per-hour monorail planned to connect American cities in the 1930s. Based on a successful German design, the American version suspended carriages from T-shaped towers 15 feet or more above

Artist's impression of the American torpedo train.

road level. Stations to serve the monorail were planned to be elevated versions of traditional railway stations. The carriages were streamlined, similar in size to those used in American subways, and ran by electricity.

It's sad that so many visionary railway pioneers of the past saw a future that was never fully realised.

Another American monorail that promised the thrills of air travel without leaving the ground.

Part II

Travel by Land

If the future as prophesised in much of the past had come to fruition, we would by now all be driving flying cars. Although the idea of flying cars was occasionally investigated, it never seriously got off the ground in the way that some inventors would have liked. Over the years, however, a great many and various other types of vehicle, almost as fanciful as the idea of a flying car, did make it into the pages of transport history, which saw vehicles driven by steam, petrol, electricity and, on rare occasions, by wind. What's more, a surprising number of those that travelled over the land didn't always run on wheels or, for that matter, along the usual idea of a road. As always, the successful designs that show how transport moved forward are interesting. But, all too often, it's the crazy ideas that never made it that prove to be the more entertaining.

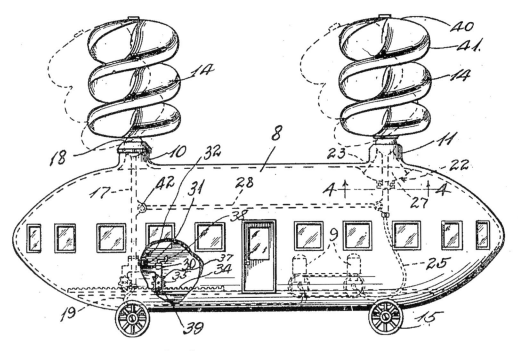

Illustration from a 1912 patent for a flying car.

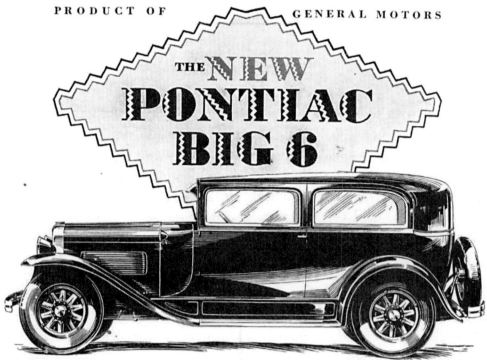

PRODUCT OF   GENERAL MOTORS

THE NEW
PONTIAC
BIG 6

2-Door Sedan ⊹ Body by Fisher

An Engineering Triumph..
A True Achievement for $745

A more practical and popular means of transport as seen in a 1929 car advertisement.

Electric Cars and Buses

The modern move away from fossil fuels and towards electricity to drive cars is not new. Electric cars were considered as far back as the early 1800s as the use of electricity became known and applied to many different fields. Innovators in Britain, France, America, Hungary and the Netherlands were among many who began turning their attentions to electric-powered vehicles. Scottish inventor Robert Anderson was among the first to introduce an electrically powered vehicle in the 1830s by the simple expedient of adding an electric motor and a large non-rechargeable battery to a normal carriage that would otherwise have been drawn by a horse. In 1865, French physicist Gaston Planté found a way to produce a rechargeable battery, making electric cars a better proposition and strongly contributing to a rise in their

From 1911, an electric car produced by the Rauch & Lang Carriage Company.

popularity. Soon, inventors and motor manufacturers all began showing an interest in this new means of transport and new ways to design cars.

Electricity versus petrol

By the turn of the twentieth century there came a boom in electric vehicles, which were seen as an improvement against horse power, the prime means of transport until that time, or steam power, which, despite seeing a great success on the railways, enjoyed less popularity in the world of road transport.

Electric vehicles were also initially seen as a direct improvement on another new means of transport beginning to emerge at that time: the petrol-driven car. The latter was expensive and difficult to drive, compared to an electric vehicle. The driver of an electric car, for example, didn't have to learn the technique of gear changing. Petrol cars also emitted nasty smelly fumes, and they needed a hand crank to start them.

Ferdinand Porsche, whose name would go on to be synonymous with racing and sports cars the world over, developed an electric car called the P1 in 1898. Around that time, Thomas Edison, one of the world's most prolific inventors, began working on battery technology to improve the use of electric cars. He was partnered in his quest by none other than American industrialist Henry Ford, who would go on to be one of the world's greatest producers of petrol-driven cars.

Ironically, it was Ford who, in the end, sounded the death knell for electric cars. In 1908, he introduced his Model T petrol-driven car, which was mass produced and relatively cheap to buy, about a third of the cost of an electric vehicle at that time. Sales increased even further with the introduction, in 1912, of an electric starter motor for petrol-driven cars, eliminating the need for the hand crank starting procedure. Petrol

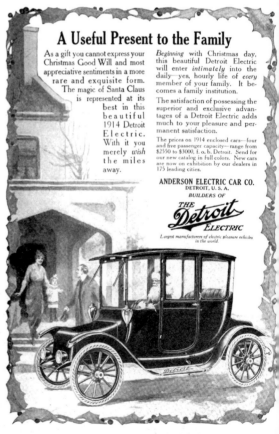

A Useful Present to the Family

As a gift you cannot express your Christmas Good Will and most appreciative sentiments in a more rare and exquisite form. The magic of Santa Claus is represented at its best in this beautiful 1914 Detroit Electric. With it you merely *wish* the miles away.

Beginning with Christmas day, this beautiful Detroit Electric will enter *intimately* into the daily—yes, hourly life of *every* member of your family. It becomes a family institution.

The satisfaction of possessing the superior and exclusive advantages of a Detroit Electric adds much to your pleasure and permanent satisfaction.

The prices on 1914 enclosed cars—four and five passenger capacity—range from $2550 to $3000, f. o. b. Detroit. Send for our new catalog in full colors. New cars are now on exhibition by our dealers in 175 leading cities.

ANDERSON ELECTRIC CAR CO.
DETROIT, U. S. A.
BUILDERS OF

THE *Detroit* ELECTRIC

Largest manufacturers of electric pleasure vehicles in the world.

Father Christmas delivers a Detroit Electric in a 1913 advertisement.

stations began springing up along popular roads, making travelling far distances easier than in an electric vehicle that needed to be returned to its home for charging at regular intervals, a situation made worse by the fact that not every home was even wired for electricity, gas being the more popular method for lighting homes.

As the popularity for petrol-driven cars increased, so the craze for electric vehicles waned. In the years ahead, there were several attempts at resurrecting electric cars, but the distances they could travel between charges was a major drawback, as was the fact that they couldn't attain high speeds. In the end, it was the start of the twenty-first century before the idea of electrically driven cars began to seem like a true reality again, and one that would eventually depose the reliance on fossil fuels. Even so, in the years between the dawn of the first electric cars and the latest revolution that finally made them a viable proposition, a lot of weird and wonderful ideas concerning the use of electronics in vehicles of all kinds came and went. Here are some of them.

Volk's electric dog cart

One of the earliest viable examples of an electric vehicle in Britain came from Magnus Volk. As an inventor who was fascinated by electricity and the many uses to which it could be put, as we have seen, Volk built Britain's first electric railway that ran along the sea front at Brighton and was also responsible for the amazing seaside electric railway that, in Brighton between 1896 and 1900, ran along railway tracks under the sea, with the carriage supported on stilt-like legs high above the water. Before that, however, in 1887, he applied his knowledge of electricity to

Magnus Volk at the steering tiller of his electric dog cart in 1887.

produce a three-wheeled dog cart, driven by an electric motor and steered by a tiller attached to the single front wheel.

His invention proved so popular in the streets of Brighton that reports of it went around the world, and when an account appeared in a German newspaper, it attracted the attention of the Sultan of Turkey, who contacted Volk with a request for one to be built for him. Volk built a four-wheeled version for the sultan, delivered it in person and, while he was in Turkey, organised the installation of electric light into the sultan's palace.

The inventor went on to build electric boats, eventually leaving Brighton and moving to London, where he operated a flotilla of electric launches on the river Thames.

La jamais contente

In April 1899, Belgian racing driver Camille Jenatzy became the first man to drive a car at more than 62 miles per hour. The car in which he achieved the record speed was electric, and it was called *La Jamais Contente*, translated as *The Never Satisfied*.

Jenatzy was born in 1868, the son of a rubber tyre manufacturer. His interest, however, was in electrical engineering, leading him to form a company to build electric taxis before becoming a racing driver. His greatest rival was Count Gaston

La Jamais Contente.

de Chasseloup-Laubat, another electric car pioneer, and the two men continually challenged one another to see who could attain the highest speeds. It was this rivalry that eventually led to Jenatzy designing and developing *La Jamais Contente*.

The torpedo-shaped car was made from a light alloy, with the driver's seat positioned high on the body. It was powered by twin electric motors connected directly to the back wheels. The batteries required to power the motors took up about half the weight of the entire vehicle, whose top speed was 65.8 miles per hour.

Jenatzy held the land speed record for more than two years, before it was beaten by French steam pioneer Léon Serpollet in a steam-driven car.

The Baker Electric Motor Vehicle Company

America was the place where electric vehicles really took off in the early years. To appreciate their growing popularity in the late nineteenth and early twentieth centuries, and to understand how, for a while, electricity was seen as the future for the automotive industry in America, look no further than the Baker Electric Motor Vehicle Company.

The business was co-founded by engineer Walter C. Baker in 1899, the year Camille Jenatzy established his land speed record in an electric car. The first Baker vehicles were little more than four-wheel frames, such as might have been pulled by a horse, but with the addition of a battery and electric motor. From there the company quickly progressed to building two-seater cars, essentially for travel in towns, where the car need not venture far from home and its battery charging point. The first cars ran on solid tyres and were steered by tillers rather than steering wheels. Before long, Baker was supplying an electric carriage to the King of Siam, complete with silver-plated metal parts, a body finished in ivory and the dashboard covered in patent leather.

By 1910, the Baker Company was making a limousine with its batteries housed under what appeared to be a conventional car bonnet and with a top speed of 30 miles per hour. The company also set out to attract a new generation of women drivers with interiors styled by eminent French fashion designer Paul Poiret. In the words of one of the company's advertisements:

> Poiret has produced a variety of exquisite effects in self-toned harmonies of gold, wine colour and shimmering greys, entirely unique in motor car interiors, which will appeal to the discriminating woman as unusually distinctive.

By the turn of the twentieth century, America had become the country most known for the production of electric cars with nearly 40,000 registered vehicles.

How the Baker Electric Motor Vehicle Company advertised its electric vehicles.

The electric share of the market showed 38 per cent of cars driven by electricity, against only 22 per cent by petrol. The remaining 40 per cent were steam driven. One of the Baker Company's advertisements of the time summed up what electric cars of this era offered:

The magnificent new Baker Coupé. Just what the public demands in a stylish yet conservative car – a genuine automobile, not an electrically driven coach. It has increased roominess; full limousine back; longer wheel base; graceful, low-hung body lines, with both interior and exterior conveniences and appointments which have set a new mark in motor car refinement. Lever steer from the rear seat or wheel steer from the front. The front seats revolve – face forward or turnabout.

The thought of the driver turning his seat around to face passengers steering the car from the back seat is one to make the mind boggle

With the outbreak of the First World War in 1914 and America's entry into the hostilities in 1917, manufacturing diminished, but Baker continued to build and sell electric cars well into the 1920s.

Hybrids hit the road

The craze for hybrid vehicles that use a mixture of petrol and electrical power is nothing new, although early versions didn't quite work like their modern equivalents. Take, for example, a hybrid engine car for which a patent was granted in 1914. It was for an open-topped car which, to all outward appearances, looked like a normal petrol-driven vehicle. Under the bonnet, however, there was a power plant consisting of a 10-horsepower engine and a 5-kilowatt dynamo. The petrol-driven engine powered the dynamo, which drove an electric motor that propelled the car. When the car was not running at its maximum speed of between 25 and 30 miles per hour, the surplus power generated by the dynamo was diverted to storage batteries, which drove the car for about 20 miles before they needed to be recharged.

A hybrid car from c.1914, with the power plant that was contained beneath the bonnet.

A sightseeing car designed for eighteen passengers, in use in South Africa during 1915. A 40-horsepower petrol engine drove an electric generator, which provided the power for an electric motor to drive the car and its lighting.

Unusual layouts

As the first wave of electric cars progressed, there were those who found new ways to design the traditional layout of controls. In 1915, one manufacturer suggested placing the steering wheel in the centre of the car's interior, slightly forward of two passenger seats, one each side. Brake levers were also placed each side of the steering column, so that the driver sat with the column between his legs. It was, said the makers, ideal for city travelling.

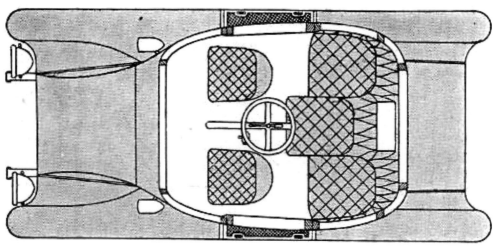

An unusual design that changed the way a steering wheel and other controls were placed in an electric car.

Trolleybuses

Time was when trams were thought to be the ultimate form of public transport. They had flanged wheels like railway engines and their carriages, and they ran on rails like railway lines, the difference being that these rails were embedded in the streets. Trams were powered by electricity picked up from a single pole that extended from the vehicle to connect with an overhead wire, with the current being harmlessly returned to earth through the rails. Trams were environmentally friendly in an age that didn't consider the environment the way that would later be the case. But they were also big and lumbering, and because they were restricted to their rails, they were unable to steer around any obstacles in their path. As more manoeuvrable cars began to appear on the roads, the inflexibility of the way trams travelled began to make them a liability. What was needed was a vehicle that could be cheaply powered by electricity, but which had the manoeuvrability of a motor bus. The answer was the trolleybus.

Having normal rubber tyres rather than metal wheels on rails, trolleybuses could steer around obstacles. Their power was picked up from a network of overhead cables, but they needed two wires, because they didn't have metal rails to complete the electric circuit as was the case with trams.

The Electromote, the first trolleybus that ran in Berlin in 1882.

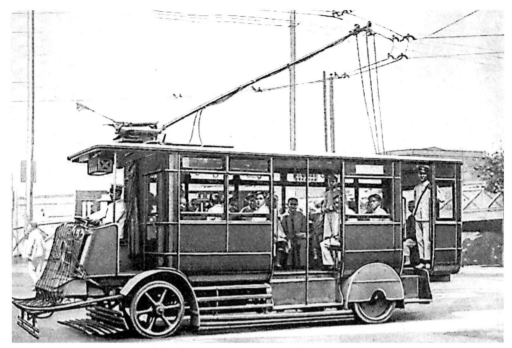

A Chinese trolleybus running in Shanghai in the 1920s.

The first trolleybus, called an Electromote, ran in Berlin in 1882. They spread throughout Europe and arrived in the UK in 1911. By the early 1920s, a form of trolleybus was running in the streets of Shanghai in China, equipped with two sections, each with its own door for first class and second class passengers. In the UK, Leeds and Bradford were the first to operate fleets. Soon there were about fifty fleets of trolleybuses running around the country, with London's red Central Area buses being the largest. Trolleybuses were similar in size and shape to a motor bus, sometimes single-deckers, but more usually double-deckers. Some styles had a total of six wheels, two at the front and four at the back. Compared to a motor bus, they had a flat front with no sign of a bonnet to house the engine. They ran smoothly and – thanks to the electric, rather than petrol or diesel engine – almost silently. They simply hummed along the road, with the occasional splutter of sparks from the overhead wires.

Some of the trolleybuses on London Transport's Central Area routes had tinted windows. This was because those vehicles had originally been built for use in South Africa. The Leyland company built twenty-five for Durban, while AEC had made eighteen for use in Johannesburg. But the Second World War intervened and the buses ended up in London, where the tinted windows, made to reduce the glare of the South African sun, were less appropriate. These trolleybuses were built with front exits for use in South Africa, although those exits had been sealed up

Trolleybuses from around the UK, top to bottom: a double-decker at Maidstone in Kent, the last of the UK single-deckers in Glasgow, and a double-decker also in Glasgow.

and replaced by a sideways seat by the time they started working on the London Transport routes. Entry and exit was by the usual red London bus means of a rear platform with a pole in the middle to hang on to.

Towns and cities that ran trolleybus routes erected complicated networks of overhead wires from which the vehicles picked up their electric current via two

A driver and conductor re-attach the poles of a London trolleybus to the overhead wires.

poles extending from the roof. Junctions where different bus numbers took different routes necessitated a set of points for the overhead wires that worked much like those on a railway track. They were operated by pulling a large brass knob that protruded from a box on one of the wire-supporting poles. To ensure every bus went in the right direction they were often run in a strict rotation with a specific bus number always following another. In this way, the conductor of each bus could reach out from his place on the rear platform and change the points ready for the next bus.

Failure to operate the points in time for the following bus, or at other times when a driver took a bend too sharply, resulted in the poles coming adrift from the wires, leaving them flailing about in the air. That was when the driver and conductor took on extra duties as pole catchers. Together they removed a long pole from under the bus and, wrestling it into an upright position, they hooked the poles and re-attached them to the overhead wires before continuing their journey.

In the UK, trolleybuses in and around London were withdrawn from service during the late 1950s and early 1960s, leaving more than twenty other locations that ran services around the country until the early 1970s. Mostly they were replaced by diesel-driven buses. Today, when everyone is being encouraged to replace their petrol, and, even worse, diesel cars, vans and lorries with electric vehicles, it seems strange to hear of a time when electricity was replaced by diesel as the preferred means of transport.

The Power of Pedals

Think of pedal-powered vehicles and you think of bicycles. But before bicycles, there were velocipedes, a word taken from the Latin for 'fast foot', and unlike bicycles, they were by no means restricted to two wheels. Three and four wheels were common and even one-wheeled contraptions were tried.

One-wheeled wonders

Imagine a huge wheel whose diameter was around the height of the average man. Inside this wheel the rider sat with his feet in stirrups and his hands on, not pedals, but a crank attached by belts to a small driving wheel on the interior circumference of the large wheel. As the rider hand-turned the crank, the large wheel began to revolve, while the mechanism allowed the rider to remain upright in its centre. Direction was controlled by the way the rider leaned while the vehicle was in motion.

The Flying Yankee, a one-wheeled way of getting around in 1869.

One-wheeled wonders like the Flying Yankee, patented by its inventor Richard C. Hemming in 1869, were more popular than might be imagined, although in truth there were probably more designs in theory than there were vehicles actually built. Nevertheless, the concept survived and, in later years, petrol-driven engines were even added.

The idea of one-wheeled transport filtered down to children's toys in 1915 with the invention of a hoop cycle. It consisted of a pipe welded into the shape of a large hoop, with a seat suspended from it on rollers so that the hoop could

Some of the many means of pedal-powered transport available to the public in the 1880s.

revolve while the seat remained stationary. Two small wheels behind kept the machine upright when not in motion and when beginning the ride. Then, as the rider scooted it along the road, leaning forward caused the stabilising wheels to lift clear of the ground so that travel was purely by means of the hoop. While it was suggested that the device could be used to coast down small hills, the manufacturers pointed out the inadvisability of its use on long steep hills where the rider might too easily lose control.

Two-wheeled bicycles

Previous to the advent of pedals to propel different means of transport, riders straddled a wooden frame with a wheel front and back and simply scooted themselves along the road. When pedals first appeared they were attached directly to one wheel, usually the front one. A popular style involved one very large front wheel with pedals attached linked to handlebars and a frame for the saddle which culminated in a smaller wheel, about a quarter the size of the front wheel, at the back. By now, in the mid-1870s, the term velocipede was beginning die out and be replaced with the word bicycle, and this style of high-wheel bicycle was epitomised by the Penny Farthing. The name was based on the old English pre-decimal currency, which contained a penny (of which there twelve to the shilling, with twenty shillings to the pound) and a farthing (a quarter the value of a penny). The two coins were of very different sizes, just like the front and back wheels of the appropriately named bicycle.

The hoop cycle was made for children.

Bicycle racing on a Penny Farthing.

The Eagle Bicycle Company swapped the positions of the large and small wheels for safer cycling.

Although the large front wheel helped increase the machine's speed and give a smoother ride over rough roads, the vehicle was difficult to mount and dismount, while hitting an object in its path could easily cause the Penny Farthing to rotate around its front wheel, pitching the rider head-first into the road with his legs trapped under the handlebars.

The American Eagle Bicycle Company was one of those who set out to correct that design fault by switching the front and back wheels. In their bicycle, the back wheel was the larger of the two and held the pedals. The rider sat above this to pedal, and steered by means of the smaller wheel in front. The company's advertisements made great play of their machine's safety, strength and speed, illustrating one of their bicycles being safely ridden alongside someone on a Penny Farthing being pitched over the front wheel and about to come into painful contact with the road. 'Old habits die hard,' claimed the wording on the poster.

Three-wheeled tricycles

Three-wheeled cycles began to be sold from the 1860s onwards.

Side by side with two-wheeled bicycles, a new craze began to grow in popularity for three-wheeled tricycles. The first three-wheeled tricycles, with one wheel at the front and two behind, became popular in the 1860s, at first with pedals situated on the front wheel. At this time, however, pedals were starting to vanish from front or back wheels and be placed instead between them, linked to the wheels by a chain. By the 1870s, the newly created chain drives were being used to power either the front or back wheels. Because of the ease of mounting, dismounting and the lessened likelihood of falling off a tricycle, compared to a bicycle, tricycles became particularly popular with lady riders, who might have heeded advertisements of the time for corsets specially designed for them. Before long, extra seats began to appear so that couples could ride together on the same machine. These were known as Sociables.

Four-wheeled quadricycles

Quadricycles were popular with couples.

The addition of an extra seat became even more popular with the manufacture of quadricycles that used four wheels, though not always in the most obvious places. Rather than use four equally-sized wheels one on each corner of the vehicle, many four-wheelers took on a design that used two large wheels, one each side of the rider or riders, and two more smaller wheels, one at the front and one at the back. The larger wheels were driven by pedals, the front wheel was used for steering and the rear wheel acted as a stabiliser. The riders usually sat one in front of the other, often a man at the back providing the pedalling power with a lady passenger in front.

Cycles for road and river

In 1893, a tricycle was designed to be capable of transporting its rider along a road or over water. The Road and River Cycle took a three-wheel tricycle of the two large wheels at the back and one smaller one at the front design, and fitted it with two small boats between the rider and the large back wheels, which were equipped with paddles attached to the spokes. When the rider reached a river or lake, he simply carried on cycling. The boats kept him afloat and pedalling the paddles on the back wheels propelled him across the water.

Multicycle for the blind

In 1909, an English institution for the blind acquired several multicycles so that its members could take outside exercise safely. The multicycles were cable of carrying up to thirteen blind cyclists for peddling purposes with one sighted leader at the front for steering. The machine consisted of pairs of wheels, each mounted on an independent axle and attached by a bar to the pair in front. In this way it was made easy for the multi-pedalled multicycle to turn when driven along winding paths.

Blind cyclists peddled the multicycle, while a sighted driver steered.

Sailing cycles

A wind-powered bicycle with sail.

Designed for riding on a beach, but said to be equally at home on the road, the bicycle with a sail that found favour in the late 1900s comprised a standard bicycle with a long board on each side, to which was fixed a sale much like that on a yacht. The sailing cyclist had to learn not just to balance on two wheels in the normal way but also to anticipate the direction of the wind and the angle into it at which the cycle had to be aimed, a specially difficult manoeuvre when turning. Because the mainsail was on a boom that could swing left and right, care had also to be taken not to let the movement overbalance the cycle at slow speeds.

Cycloplanes

The cycloplane, on show at a 1909 aerial show in London, wasn't, as its name suggested, a machine to allow bicycles to take to the air. It was in fact a boxlike contraption designed to be mounted on a

The cycloplane, designed for more speed on a bicycle.

cycle above the rider's head by means of a pole attached to the crossbar. The idea was that, as the cyclist moved along the road, air would get under the device, giving it lift in the way an aircraft takes off. It wouldn't be enough to raise the bicycle off the ground, but it would make the machine lighter, resulting in more speeds from the peddling rider.

Rowing cycle

The Four-Wheeled Auto Cycle, which appeared briefly in France in 1922, was like a cross between a velocipede and a rowing boat. The rider sat on a sliding seat at the centre of the four wheels and propelled himself along the road by means of two handles that operated similar to the oars of a boat. In this way it was reputed to be able to reach speeds of 18 miles per hour.

Rowing cycles take to the road.

Propeller-driven bicycles

In the early twentieth century pedals were not used just to drive wheels. In one vehicle, pedals drove a large propeller fixed to a bicycle frame and mounted on sledge-type runners. In this way, the vehicle could run at speed across ice, while small castor wheels embedded in the base of the runners also allowed the propeller bike to be driven, albeit at slower speeds, along a road.

Propeller-driven cycle on sledge runners and castors.

Flying bikes

In 1925, an American farm labourer built a glider attached to a bicycle. It was launched by cycling fast down the side of a hill, while steering was accomplished by wires stretching from the outer tips of the wings to the bicycle's handlebars.

A bicycle made to fly – if the rider could peddle fast enough.

'Now every boy can get the feel of the air,' claimed an advertisement for the Glide-O-Bike in 1930. The device comprised a set of wings that could rapidly be attached to the front of a normal bicycle. When sufficient speed was reached, the front wheel would lift from the ground, with the rear wheel remaining on the ground to allow

A 1930 advertisement for the Glide-O-Bike.

pedal power. Advertisements claimed that the Glide-O-Bike would bank, stall, ground-loop etc., giving its young riders the thrills of flying without leaving the ground. It was, claimed the advertising, 'the first time in the history of aviation that so much fun is placed within the reach of everyone who rides a bicycle'.

A bicycle made for four

Charles Steinlauf was an American bicycle inventor who came up with several weird and wonderful designs. The strangest was for a family bicycle made for himself, his wife, their son and daughter. It was a two-tier bicycle with Steinlauf riding and peddling on top as he steered by means of a large car steering wheel, his son also peddling at the rear and his daughter precariously balanced in a seat on the handlebars over the front wheel. His wife sat sideways below Charles and between their children, incongruously using a sewing machine. The sewing machine was operated by a treadle and it was this that kept the bicycle from falling over when it was standing still. Steinlauf and his family rode their bicycle around Chicago in 1939. They called it the *Goofybike*.

Charles Steinlauf and his family take to the road on a bicycle made for four.

The rise of the motorcycle

The transition from pedal power to engine power began in the mid-nineteenth century, although many early attempts at building a motorcycle involved little more than adding an engine to an already established make of cycle or velocipede, and in the early days, many still retained their pedals.

In 1860, French blacksmith Pierre Michaux found a way to fit a velocipede with a steam engine. Later, in America, better coal-fired boilers added more power to Michaux's original designs. In 1881, American inventor Lucius Copeland managed to reduce the size of the engine and steam boiler so that it could be attached to a bicycle capable of reaching 12 miles per hour.

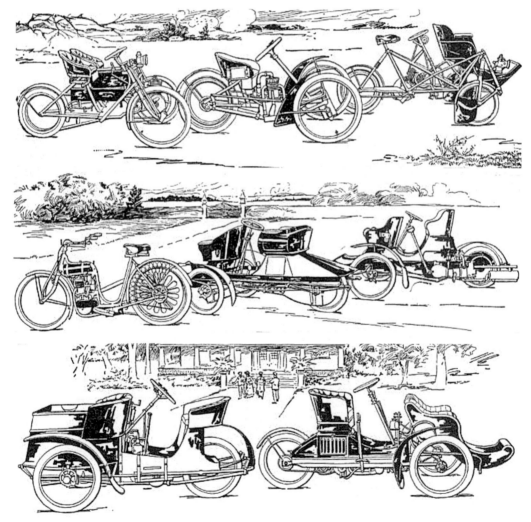

Early motorbikes as they were transformed from pedal to engine power. Top row, left to right: Thomas Tricar, Barnes Tricar, Sharp Tricar; centre row, left to right: Roc Woman's Motor Cycle, Rexette, Arielette; bottom row, left to right: Bat Tricar, Humber Tricar.

Around that time, England's International Inventions Exhibition introduced the forerunners of what would become today's motorcycles, although they had three wheels, not two. In fact, three wheels was the norm for many early models, made with two wheels at the front and one at the rear. Saddles as we know them today were rare as well, with many models placing their riders in the kinds of seats more like those seen in early motor cars, with passengers riding in a seat in front of the driver. Many early models incorporated pedals as a way to start petrol-driven engines, and also as a back-up if the engine failed.

In a short time the now traditional look of motorcycles with two wheels and passengers carried on a pillion behind the rider started to become the norm. By the outbreak of the First World War in 1914, motorcycle manufacture had spread around the world, with the war itself responsible for much of their popularity as dispatch riders and those involved with communications that had previously relied on horse power began to make the switch to motorcycles.

Not every motorcycle of the time followed a traditional design. One propeller-driven cycle looked at first sight more like an aircraft without wings. That's because, although this was a motorcycle, it was constructed almost entirely from old aeroplane parts, complete with a rear-mounted propeller that drove it forwards. Braking was achieved by two hardwood reels that pressed as hard as possible against the rear wheels. The strange vehicle was first seen in 1922.

A motorcycle made from aeroplane parts, complete with propeller.

A 1927 advertisement for Harley Davidson motorcycles.

The period between the end of the First World War in 1918 and the beginning of the Second World War in 1939 saw nearly 100 motorcycle manufacturers starting business in the UK alone. Between them they created the motorcycle as it is known today, something very different from the designs and styles of the first models around fifty years before.

Unusual Petrol, Steam and Wind Power Vehicles

While petrol was the most popular fuel for cars right from the earliest days, there were those who sought different methods of driving a car, usually along a road, but sometimes along a railway track.

Cars on tracks

In the early 1900s an American inventor came up with an idea to run cars on tracks. Unlike railways in which the engine's flanged wheels run on top of metal tracks, these would be made of concrete and constructed in an 'L' shape. The car's wheels ran along the horizontal base of the track while its vertical side kept them in place. The cars that used the tracks, however, needed to be converted with small guide wheels that travelled in front of the vehicle in contact with the sides of the tracks to automatically steer the car.

Concrete tracks to keep a car on the right road.

With concrete cheaper than the iron used on railways, the road tracks could be manufactured on the spot as they were laid along the roads. It was suggested that laying the tracks would make work for convicted criminals.

Wind wagons

Airship technology was the thinking behind the wind wagon conceived by a New York inventor who had been working on propellers for airships when he decided it would be just as easy to make a propeller drive a car along the road. The vehicle he built was made of wood and used three bicycle type wheels, two at the rear and a

A propeller-driven car could travel on land or water.

steering wheel at the front. At the rear, a 6-foot propeller, driven by a petrol engine, pushed the vehicle along the road at speeds of up to 30 miles per hour.

Meanwhile in France, another inventor found a way to attach a propeller to a motorcycle. In this case, the propeller was mounted in front and so pulled the vehicle along the road, rather than pushing it. Later, the same inventor added a petrol engine-driven propeller to a bicycle and attained reported speeds of up to 49 miles per hour.

Vehicles such as these were by no means confined to running on roads. Since the motive power was courtesy of a propeller rather than an engine connected to the wheels, it worked just as well for driving the vehicle across water, with its redundant

Equally at home on land or water and seen from the front and back, a propeller-driven car from America.

wheels roped to a barge and a rudder connected to the car's steering wheel for guidance.

Whether on the road or over water, an American automobile made in 1926 was equally at home. Looking like a cross between a boat, a luxury car and a small aeroplane, it was driven by an aeroplane engine that drove a huge propeller mounted on the back. Air-tight pontoons under the running boards kept it buoyant on water, when the front wheels acted as steering devices. On dry land the vehicle ran on four rubber-tyred wheels and was said to work just as well over ice and through snow.

When propeller-driven cars did run along roads, they were known for their preponderance to badly frighten horses.

Homes in cars

A car for living in and on top of in 1908.

In Europe, by the end of the first decade of the twentieth century, touring was all the rage. But why stop at a hotel, when you can take your hotel with you? So began a European craze for motor vehicles that you did more than drive; you lived in them as well – or on top of them. In Europe they became known as caravan cars, or just caravans. In America they called them house cars. The size of a small bus, the vehicles contained sleeping births for six people and were fully equipped with a kitchen at the rear so that cooking odours did not reach the passengers. Such odours were unlikely to worry passengers during travel, though, because they sat in the open air in seats on the roof.

Meanwhile, across the Atlantic, in Florida a businessman also equipped his car for not just travelling, eating and sleeping in, but as a mobile office, complete with library. The interior was fitted out in mahogany, with silk curtains at the windows, electric light and other modern conveniences.

Also in America, a senator who was supervising the building of a major highway through his home state in 1911 took his living accommodation with him, thanks to his combined car and tent. The car was long enough to incorporate a 6-foot long mattress with storage cupboards on either side. When making camp, however, a tent made of waterproof balloon silk was unfolded to extend the width of the car on each side enough to allow living accommodation with

A 1909 businessman's touring office.

internal curtains that divided the car-cum-tent into three compartments. Storage boxes built into the vehicle contained various domestic items, including bedding and even a small refrigerator.

As the craze for touring in mobile homes increased, so the vehicles got bigger and more comprehensive until they began to be known, in America, as auto-bungalows.

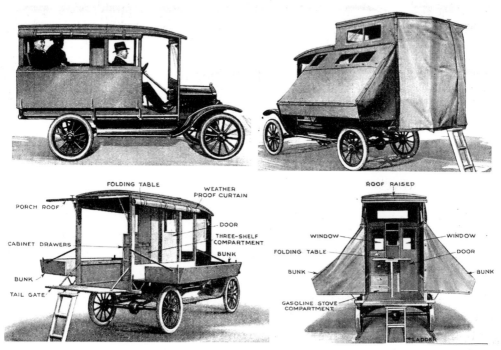

The versatility of an early autobungalow.

One such, built by a retired farmer at a cost of $16,000 in 1921, was used to transport his friends and family on a two-year trip. It began life as a standard four-wheeled motor truck with a new 30-foot-long body added, which resulted in a good third of it overhanging the rear wheels. The living quarters took up 20 feet of the interior, with a kitchen, couches, easy chairs, folding beds, a dining room table and other necessary furnishings and comforts. The kitchen was equipped with a gas stove, refrigerator and hot water tank. Toilet facilities and a shower were also included. Storage space beneath the vehicle held the family's luggage.

Also in 1921, rather than converting a road vehicle into a home, one American inventor converted a house into a road vehicle. It looked like a small bungalow, complete with a front porch and folding stairs, windows, a pitched roof and chimney, but with four wheels. The window at the front of the building was the windscreen, with flower pots each side and headlights above. Inside, the building-cum-vehicle offered a folding bed and table, an icebox, pantry, sink with running water fed from a water tank on the roof, a stove for cooking and electric lighting. Four people comfortably lived and travelled in the house on wheels.

Some American auto-bungalows were not so much homes built into cars, but more cars built into homes.

Funerals on wheels

If you can put a house in a car, why not a chapel? The automobile funeral car, at nearly 23 feet long, contained everything needed for a successful mobile funeral. Equipped with electric light, it held space inside for the coffin, compartments for flowers and seating for up to thirty-six mourners, taking the place of a hearse and as many as nine attendant cars. Although capable of 14 miles per hour, it was more usually driven to a funeral at about 8 miles per hour. On arrival at the graveside, it could be transformed into a chapel for the service. The funeral car was the brainchild of an American inventor in 1910, who claimed it to be the only one of its type in the world.

Everything needed for a funeral … on wheels.

The bigger the better

Two big cars from America
(above) and France (below) in
1912.

'All the comforts of the parlour' was the way this super-size vehicle for fifty-three passengers was described in 1930.

Not every car of the early 1900s conformed to the usual two or four seats. Some were built to seat far more. In America, a sightseeing vehicle for tourists was produced in the style of an elongated touring car that seated sixteen people. In France, the Inspector of Finances took delivery of what, in 1912, was believed to be the biggest touring car in the world. It had a wheelbase of nearly 17 feet, seated eight passengers in a limousine style of body and its rear wheels were equipped with twin tyres. To house the 160-horsepower engine, the car's bonnet took up nearly half the overall length of the car, with the driver sitting in an open-air compartment between the bonnet and the passengers.

Railway engine car

The cross-country locomotive, resembling a train running on the road.

Was it a car, was it a railway engine, or was it a bit of both? Actually it was a car, built to look like a railway engine. The vehicle, which appeared in 1921, used a conventional petrol engine. The driving rods from the engine to the car wheels were in fact air pumps that filled a tank behind the driver for inflating the tyres and blowing a whistle. Domes on the top of the body were for cooling the engine and filling the petrol tank. What appeared to be the train's funnel concealed the radiator cap. The inventor called his strange hybrid vehicle a cross-country locomotive.

Cars without wheels

Given the need to climb steep hills, uneven terrain, or a mixture of both, legs beat wheels every time. So why not equip a car with legs in place of wheels? That was the thinking behind a German motor manufacture who demonstrated just such a vehicle on a steep slope as it climbed to the top of a 45-degree gradient before descending down the other side. In fact, the 'legs' were more like the kind of runners found on a sledge. Three such runners were arranged in parallel on the base of the vehicle, all three resting on the ground when the car was not in motion. When the motor was started, two of the runners remained stationary, while others lifted, moved forward and dropped back to the ground. The action was then repeated with the runners on the opposite side of the car. In this way, the car moved forward,

A car on leg-like runners from Germany, ideal for climbing mountains.

while it was always standing on two sets of runners. German military authorities in 1914 considered use of vehicles of this type to transport guns, ammunition and other supplies over rough country.

Power scooters

Anyone familiar with the kind of scooters ridden by children in the 1950s will be conversant with this more adult version of the same idea that came to light around 1914, predating today's current craze for similar appliances by 100 years.

The design was very much like a traditional child's scooter, comprising a platform on which the rider stood upright with a single wheel at each end and a long steering pillar attached to the front wheel for steering. The difference with this grown-up scooter was that a small petrol engine was built into the front wheel. It was started by propelling the scooter with one foot on the platform and one foot on the

Scooters for grown-ups, all the rage in 1914.

ground, then placing both feet on the platform as the engine sprang into life. The motor was fed by fuel stored in the hollow steering pillar and it was claimed that the scooter, suitable for both men and women, could reach speeds of 20 miles per hour and operated at 100 miles per gallon of petrol.

The cyclecar

As the First World War ended, petrol shortages in Europe turned inventors' thoughts towards building more economical means of transport. Out of this thinking came the cyclecar for a single driver. It consisted of a light body with two motorcycle wheels at the front and a small rear wheel driven by the kind of two-cylinder engine

The small cyclecar.

used to convert pedal bikes into motorcycles. The engine was started by the driver using a push pedal before boarding the car. Aircraft engineering was the influence behind he cyclecar's streamlined body, while its spring suspension was adapted from the shock-absorbing principles of aeroplane landing gear. The vehicles were claimed to be capable of a sustained speed of 20 miles per hour and, in trials, one of the tiny cars attained a speed of 47 miles per hour.

The torpedo car

The Italian torpedo car.

Advances in the theory of aerodynamics and knowledge of the effects of wind resistance resulted in a torpedo-shaped car built in Italy in 1915. Equipped with a 50-horsepower engine, the bare chassis of the car reached speeds of 66 miles per hour on a test track. The addition of the peculiarly shaped body, rounded at the front and pointed at the rear, added an extra 14 miles per hour to its top speed. Over the same track and in similar conditions, the vehicle attained a new top speed of 80 miles per hour. The unusual style aroused some interest from the Italian motor industry in Milan, but did little to steer manufacturers away from building the more traditional shapes of automobiles.

A folding car

A car that could be folded to less than half its width to get it through the door of a house was pioneered in England in 1928. The car, however, did not have an engine. Instead, it was operated by pedals and had both hand and foot brakes. It was reputed to have been driven at speeds of up to 30 miles per hour.

Front-wheel drive

A sleek design aided by the advent of front-wheel drive.

A new era in car design was ushered in during the 1920s when the advantages of front-wheel drive were utilised. With the more traditional back-wheel drive used by most car manufacturers, the drive shaft from the engine at the front to the wheels at the back presented a major obstacle in streamlining sleek designs. With the advent of front-wheel drive, new low-hung cars with teardrop-shaped bodies came into being. New designs in England and on the Continent offered sleek bodies with low centres of gravity, which had the added advantage of being able to take turns at high speed with less a tendency to turn over even in serious skids.

Off-road driving

Mud was no obstacle to this car with caterpillar tracks.

For driving through mud or other environments unfriendly to the traditional car, an English-designed car of the 1920s featured a caterpillar tread on each side that could be raised or lowered as necessary when the terrain became too difficult for the car's normal four wheels. When the caterpillar unit was lowered, the main wheels were elevated clear of the ground.

Palaces on wheels from around the world. Top to bottom: American, French, English and an articulated version from America.

Palaces on wheels

The 1920s saw a significant acceleration around the world of tourists abandoning trains in favour of road travel in enormous vehicles that offered passengers all the comforts more usually associated with travelling by rail.

In America, California – known for its tourist industry – was where one of these monster cars-cum-buses emanated. Capable of carrying twenty passengers, the vehicle featured eight wheels, four at the front and four at the back. All four front wheels were used for steering and all four back wheels drove the vehicle and housed its brakes. Each of the five cross seats inside the huge cabin had its own door, with another two doors for the driver. It did 10 miles to the gallon.

Meanwhile in France, elaborate vehicles of this type were being dubbed 'palaces on wheels' as they ran from Calais in northern France to the Riviera in the south over a six-day trip. Seats to hold two people each were placed at the front of the bus, with an aisle between them, while an eight-seat arrangement was set out around the rear in a 'U' shape. All seats were luxuriously upholstered. Nickel-plated fittings on the seats included cigarette lighters and fold-down trays. Electric lighting was mounted in the roof. Outside, the front and rear of the bus were fitted with the latest in safety devices with indicator arrows to show intended turns. The arrows, red at the back, green at the front, were lit at night and, simultaneous with their being activated, a horn sounded to attract the attention of other drivers. Another safety factor consisted of safety valves attached to the rims of the wheels so that, if air pressure in a tyre dropped below a certain level, an explosive charge alerted the driver.

English vehicles, similar to their French counterparts, seated twenty-six passengers in two compartments. In the front compartment, seats were arranged across the cabin. In the rear compartment, couch-like seats were arranged along the sides and around the back. Separate entrances were used for each compartment. Outside, a locker ran along the entire length of the bus for passenger luggage. In a second English version of luxury buses, the passenger seats were in the form of revolving armchairs, and tables could also be erected between them.

In America, as many as eighty bus lines were in operation in Minnesota during 1922. Similar monster buses were also built and used in Scotland, Norway, Switzerland, the French Alps and the Pyrenees.

The raindrop car

A German car designer considered the raindrop to be the ultimate shape when it came to streamlining and the least resistance to wind. The result was a new design of car body that made its appearance at a 1922 Berlin motor show. Seats were

The raindrop-shaped car, built to withstand wind resistance.

arranged in single file down the centre of the car, with the driver in front and two passengers behind. The engine was at the back over the rear axle. The car was said to be capable of speeds of up to 75 miles per hour.

Automatic steering

By the mid-1930s, some saw the speeds attainable by road cars as being too fast for safety, as human reflexes struggled to react fast enough to keep a car's steering straight at high velocities. How much better it would be if the driver could leave all the driving functions to a vehicle's electronic brain.

How the self-steering car might have looked in action.

To make that work, the road would need to be equipped with steel mirrors under rubber hoods aligned down the centre of the lane along which the car travelled. On the specially equipped car, a large, bright spot lamp mounted on the front would have its beam directed at a lens used to concentrate the light on the mirrors in the road, from where the light was reflected back to photo electric sensors in the front of the car. What the inventors called a mechanical-electrical brain would then swing into action to sense if the car was veering away from a straight path and so correct the steering. If the

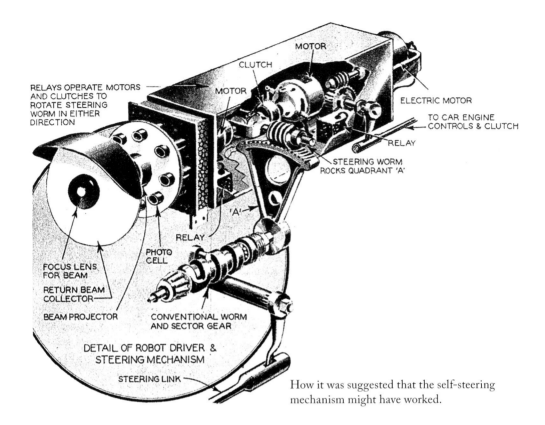

MOTOR

CLUTCH

MOTOR

RELAYS OPERATE MOTORS
AND CLUTCHES TO
ROTATE STEERING
WORM IN EITHER
DIRECTION

ELECTRIC MOTOR

TO CAR ENGINE
CONTROLS & CLUTCH

RELAY

STEERING WORM
ROCKS QUADRANT 'A'

'A'

RELAY

PHOTO
CELL

FOCUS LENS
FOR BEAM

RETURN BEAM
COLLECTOR

BEAM PROJECTOR

CONVENTIONAL WORM
AND SECTOR GEAR

DETAIL OF ROBOT DRIVER &
STEERING MECHANISM

STEERING LINK

How it was suggested that the self-steering
mechanism might have worked.

car drifted left, the sensors on the right of the car activated the steering to swing it
to the right; if the car drifted right, the sensors on the left of the car activated the
steering to swing it to the left.

In this way, the car could operate at speed along a path dictated by the mirrors set
in the road, and would continue to do so without any input from the driver.

Flying cars

Although the prophesised future for the motor car was for it to take to the air, it
obviously never really happened, although there were those who gave it a go. The
patent filed by American inventor H.J. Snook in 1912 showed an enclosed body
where a driver and passengers could sit and, above that, twin helical propellers,
looking like gigantic corkscrews to lift the car off the ground and then propel it
through the air.

What looked a lot like a small speedster type of motor car with huge propellers
mounted above it earned the vehicle proposed by two Argentine inventors in 1921
the title of flying car. It was, however, better classified as a small helicopter. The
body of the machine did indeed look like that of a small racing car complete with

four wheels, but the propellers above were nothing like anything seen on road or race track. Two propellers, one above the other, revolved in opposite directions. Each consisted of six sets of twin blades, making twelve in all. The sheer size of the twelve blades, compared to the body below, gave the power required for lift. The motive power came from an engine incorporated into the body. In tests, the inventor demonstrated how it could take off vertically, fly forward and hover on the spot.

A flying car design from Argentina.

At the 1922 Paris Aero Show, a biplane was shown with wings that folded to turn the aircraft into a street-going automobile. The wings were hinged to the plane fuselage, and when folded, the vehicle was about the size of a bus and able to run along the streets powered by a 10-horsepower engine. Once on an airfield, the wings were unfolded and a second 30-horsepower motor took over to provide the power. The aircraft performed well at the air show and subsequently attracted a lot of attention running along the boulevards of Paris.

Half car, half aeroplane, a 1927 design from Germany resulted in a small plane with a cabin similar to that of a sedan car of the time, complete with large windows rarely seen in conventional aircraft. The flying car was propelled by two

On the road or in the air, a French invention that was equally at home in both.

A British flying car advertised as ideal for tourists of the future.

motorcycle engines that turned propellers mounted on the front of the wings. The wheels, used for landing, were mounted on two stubby winglike extensions from the base of the body, but could be retracted to fold up at right angles. In this way they and the body extensions on which they were mounted would act like floats to facilitate landing on water.

Equally at home on the road, on water or even in the air, a strange vehicle from 1928.

Only slightly more practical was a strange vehicle on show at a British exhibition in 1928, where it was hailed as the ideal transport for tourists of the future. A small cabin held several people, it ran on wheels along the road, floated when driven into water and had wings that folded out from the sides with a tail and rudder at the rear, plus two propellers that allowed it to fly. It was claimed that it took very little time to change the vehicle from one mode of transport to another.

Then came the *Triphibion*, described in a 1936 copy of *Mechanics and Handicraft* magazine. Here was a small one-seater vehicle, about the size of a motorcycle sidecar, equipped with an engine to drive four large bicycle-size wheels. Above the driver's head a large circular parachute-like canopy was suspended on struts. History does not record much about how the *Triphibion* worked, but the general idea seemed to be that as the vehicle was driven forwards the canopy would act like a hot-air balloon and lift it from the ground. Controls within the cockpit would then allow the driver to rock the canopy in different orientations as a method of steering.

The inventor's name was Constantino Vlachos and it was he who took the *Triphibion* on its first

The *Triphibion*, doomed before it even started.

and last journey in Washington DC. Unfortunately, whatever was being used to heat the air under the canopy in an effort to make it rise caused the vehicle to burst into flames long before lift-off. A passing policeman and another member of the public managed to stop the vehicle and pull Vlachos from the flames. He was taken to hospital with severe burns, leaving behind the ruins of his *Triphibion*, which was destined never to travel the roads again, let alone fly above them.

Thomas Finley's rocket car

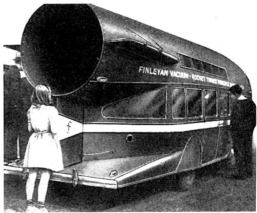

Front and back, the rocket car.

A strangely propelled vehicle built in the 1930s was part car and part airship. The car was based on a Ford motor car chassis, onto which inventor Thomas Finley built a huge tubular structure incorporating a large two-bladed propeller, designed to suck air in at the front and expel it from the rear. Around town, the vehicle could be driven in the usual way. But once on the open road, the propeller was engaged to drive the car at speed. The design had the further advantage of giving the entire vehicle a slight lift from the ground, which ensured a smoother ride than normal. Fins added to the rear kept the vehicle stable during its rocket-like travel.

Turbine-driven car

The power of the wind provided the motive power for another car planned in the 1930s.

The wind-powered turbo car.

The small two-seater was dominated by a huge wind turbine cleverly designed to utilise energy from the wind irrespective of which way the car was facing or the wind was blowing. Inside the turbine housing, the rotating wind-driven blades were connected directly to the rear wheels via gears and shafts. Batteries were also incorporated to store excess energy from the turbine and this could be used to drive an electric motor when the vehicle was not in a position to capture the power of the wind.

The inventor was Soviet scientist K.E. Tsiolkovsky, who had a model of his invention built. It is doubtful that a full-size wind-driven vehicle was produced.

One-wheel car and bus

Most road vehicles were equipped with at least two wheels, and preferably a minimum of three or four. The Dynasphere, shown in 1932 by English electrical engineer and inventor Dr John Purves, had only one.

It was enormous and the driver sat inside it. Tracks ran around the inner circumference of the gigantic wheel, to which a motor was geared. If the weight of the motor and/or its driver had been too light, the mechanism would have caused both to climb up the inner surface of the wheel. But the weight of the motor and its driver meant that they remained parallel with the ground, while the wheel was dragged forwards. Two versions were made, one using a

Dr Purves's Dynasphere, driven by his son in 1932.

petrol engine and a second one that ran by electricity. Speeds of up to 30 miles per hour were attained with a driver and one passenger on board.

In 1935, Dr Purves took the concept a major step forward and used it as the basis for a motor bus to carry a driver and passengers inside a small cabin surrounded by the huge wheel. The bus was driven by the large wheel in the same way as a smaller motor drove the Dynasphere, but with the addition of four more small wheels. Two wheels, front and back, were used only when stopping and starting. Two more wheels, one on each side of the bus, could be lifted and lowered to aid steering. As either wheel was lifted, the entire apparatus tipped to the side, which caused the vehicle to turn. A stabilising fin at the rear kept the bus level at high speeds.

How the one-wheel idea was suggested for use in a motor bus.

Both the Dynasphere and the bus proved successful in theory, but the practicality of steering and braking meant neither achieved the success for which Dr Purves might have hoped.

The Dymaxion

Buckminster Fuller was an American inventor, architect, author and futurist – the ideal man to come up with a vehicle like the Dymaxion, which he introduced in 1933. Its name was derived from a contraction of the words dynamic maximum tension. The long, tube-like body, reminiscent more of a Zeppelin airship than a road-going vehicle, was designed for its aerodynamic fuel efficiency. It was reckoned it would use only half the fuel of any comparative vehicle of the time.

The Dymaxion had three wheels, front-wheeled drive from the two at the front, and one at the back, which was used for steering. Since this wheel could be locked at 90 degrees, the vehicle could turn and revolve in a very tight space. In place of a rear-view mirror, it used a periscope to look backwards along the top of the body. A

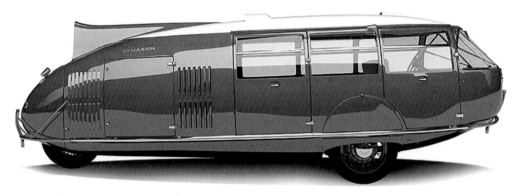

The short-lived Dymaxion.

driver and up to eleven passengers could be transported at speeds of up to 90 miles per hour, but because of its style and shape, it needed a highly trained operator to drive it.

At first, the vehicle was received with a great deal of enthusiasm, and there were plans for it to be built by Chrysler as orders came in from the likes of aviation pioneer Amelia Earhart and musician Leopold Stokowski. The enthusiasm was short-lived. Only three prototypes were ever built. The first was involved in a collision with another car, which caused it to roll over and the driver was killed. Of the three original prototypes, one was broken up for scrap, another destroyed by fire, and the third wound up dumped in a farmer's field, where it was used as a chicken coop.

Part III

Travel Over and Under Water

Over the years, many different types of craft have taken to the water, either to travel over it or to sometimes travel under it. The vast majority of course were completely conventional in their designs. But there were those that differed from the norm: boats that could fly, boats that were powered by pedals like bikes, boats whose motive power came from propellers like aircraft, boats that travelled on land as well as water, boats built to travel on ice, gigantic boats, miniature boats… and who would have thought a submarine might be powered by electricity?

It might look like a car without wheels, but it's actually a vehicle that runs over water when it's frozen. It uses sledge runners in place of wheels, with the front runners attached to a conventional steering wheel. This rather fanciful idea of an ice car/boat/sleigh was envisaged by an artist in 1910.

Floating Giants

When it comes to building big, water-based means of transport have always led the way over anything built to travel on land or in the air. While history has seen large motor cars, huge aircraft and enormous trains, they all pale into insignificance against some of the gigantic ships and boats built to travel across oceans or to traverse large lakes. Among the biggest and the best was one super-size ship designed by one of the nineteenth century's greatest inventors: Isambard Kingdom Brunel.

The Great Eastern

When Isambard Kingdom Brunel built something, he built it big, and that was never more true than when he built ships. The Brunel-designed SS *Great Western* was a wooden paddle wheel steamship purpose-built for crossing the Atlantic and was the largest passenger ship in the world when launched in 1837. Then came the SS *Great Britain*, launched in 1843, to become the longest passenger ship in the world. But Brunel's most ambitious project in steamship building came with an enormous vessel that he originally called *Leviathan*, but which soon became known as the SS *Great Eastern*.

A painting of the SS *Great Eastern* on the high seas.

During preparations for The Great Exhibition, the first in a series of world fairs organised to exhibit the works and industry of the world's principal nations in 1851, Brunel had met Scottish civil engineer John Scott Russell, whom he now partnered in the *Great Eastern* project. Together they formed a proposal that was put to the Eastern Steam Navigation Company. Brunel put considerable sums of his own money into the project and Russell's engineering firm was awarded the shipbuilding contract. Work began in 1853.

Brunel was to remark at the time that he had never before put so much time, thought and labour into a project. The ship was originally designed to carry as many as 4,000 passengers on a non-stop journey from the UK to Australia, along

Part of a grinding wheel used in the construction of the SS *Great Eastern*, now on display outside the Brunel Museum in South London.

with cargo trade between England and what was then Ceylon, now Sri Lanka. As well as sails strung from six masts, steam engines were employed, attached to a screw propeller and huge paddle wheels on each side of the ship. At 22,500 tons and nearly 700 feet long, the *Great Eastern* was six times the size of any ship built up until that time. The paddle wheels were 36 feet high and the propeller was 24 feet wide. With a twin hull and iron bulkheads dividing the ship into ten water-tight compartments, she was reckoned to be unsinkable.

The ship was built at Millwall on the river Thames in London and, unlike most ships, it was built parallel to the bank of the river. Since its size would restrict the normal kind of launch in which the ship would slide down a runway into the water, the plan was to ease the ship sideways along specially constructed runways to float at high tide. Things, however, did not go to plan.

Problems arose when John Scott Russell went bankrupt. Work came to a halt until Brunel managed to raise the money to go on building the half-finished ship, despite failing to win the support of Russell's workforce. After more delays, an attempt was made to launch the hull in November 1857. Due to technical problems and the interference of crowds who had paid to watch the proceedings, the launch was a disaster. Two more attempts were made later the same month, but they failed too. With new equipment acquired to facilitate the tricky manoeuvre, the hull of

The deck of the *Great Eastern*, looking aft from one of the paddle boxes.

the *Great Eastern* was eventually launched in January 1858, and moved along the river to Deptford to be fitted out.

In an August 1859 edition of *The Illustrated London News*, a writer described the sensation of standing on the bridge between the paddle boxes and looking aft. It was noted that other normal size boats looked like toys beside the *Great Eastern* and that the tops of their masts as they passed scarcely reached the deck of the great ship. Twenty lifeboats, all equipped with their own masts and sails, were strung from davits along the sides.

A suite of luxurious saloons stretched along the length of the ship, interrupted only by the engine rooms in the centre. The saloons were in two tiers, the top tier having floors that fell short of extending their entire width, leaving a gap protected by an elegant balustrade and so allowing light to the lower tier. The cabins were arranged on both sides of this line of saloons and stretched to each side of the ship. Some cabins accommodated just two people, others had a large enough capacity for a whole family. A typical family cabin measured 18 x 7½ feet and was equipped with a table that could be extended or collapsed to different sizes, chairs that included a rocker, a washstand and twin couches along opposite walls, one of which converted into a bath. Bunks arranged along one wall could be curtained off during the day. The cabin floor was lined with oilcloth covered with Turkish rugs.

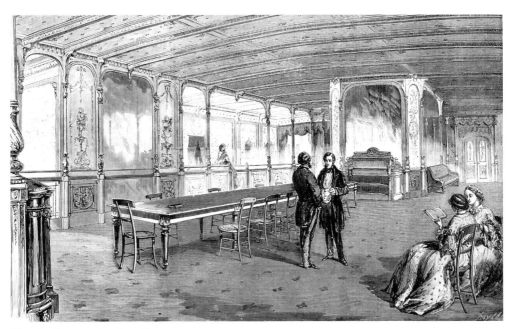

Grand saloon on the *Great Eastern*.

A family cabin on the *Great Eastern*.

By September 1859, the SS *Great Eastern* was ready for sea trials, but its first voyage ended prematurely when temporary stopcocks fitted to heaters on two funnels were inadvertently left in place, resulting in a devastating explosion that killed five men and injured others. By now, Brunel was not a well man, having suffered a stroke and collapsing on deck of the ship a few days before the trials, and it was said that news of the explosion might have accelerated his death. A heavy smoker, he was diagnosed with nephritis – a disease associated with inflammation of the kidneys – and died the same month.

Nevertheless, the *Great Eastern* did complete a few passenger-carrying transatlantic trips, finally reaching New York in June 1860, when the ship was exhibited to the public and spent a few months travelling along the East Coast of America, before returning to the UK. A year later, the *Great Eastern* made another trip across the Atlantic, by which time the American Civil War was in progress, and the ship was used to transport troops to Quebec in Canada to reinforce Canadian defences. Several more transatlantic trips were made. One hit a severe storm, disabling the ship, another ended when the ship hit an uncharted rock as it entered New York Harbour, resulting in more costly repairs. Two more trips took place in 1863, but the financial side of the journeys led to bankruptcy.

The SS *Great Eastern* was eventually sold at auction in 1864 to the Telegraph Construction and Maintenance Company, who were newly formed for the purpose

Screw engine room on the *Great Eastern*.

Cable-laying machinery aboard the *Great Eastern*.

of laying a telegraph cable under the Atlantic from the UK to America. The *Great Eastern* was about the only ocean-going vessel large enough to carry the huge length of cable necessary for the task. But even that didn't go to plan at the start. At the first attempt in 1865, having set forth from Ireland, the end of the cable was lost overboard 600 miles from Newfoundland. A new company called the Anglo-American Telegraph Company was formed and a fresh attempt made at laying the cable succeeded in July 1866.

In the end, the *Great Eastern* might have failed to spend its life doing what it had been designed as – the world's biggest passenger-carrying ship – but it eventually found its niche as a cable-laying vessel. In the following years, it was used to lay six more cables between Europe and America, and another across the Indian Ocean.

In 1866 the *Great Eastern* went on to become an exhibition ship, as it visited London and Scotland. But in 1887, the huge ship took its last voyage to Liverpool where, from 1888 to 1889, it was broken up for scrap.

Cunard's biggest ship

Six passenger decks, accommodation for 3,000 passengers and 500 crew, a dining room that could seat 500 at one time, 676 feet long and a weight of 20,000 tons – those were just some of the statistics applied to the *Carmania*, the largest turbine steamer of its time. Built by the British John Brown Company, it incorporated

Cunard's gigantic *Carmania*, which travelled the transatlantic route from 1905 to 1910.

the largest cooking facilities ever seen on a ship, staterooms that could be occupied by anything from a single individual up to an entire family, and even wireless telegraph and submarine signal telephones for the use of its passengers. Top to bottom, its six passenger decks housed: promenades and lounges; promenades, drawing rooms and staterooms; promenades, staterooms and a domed saloon; the dining saloon; second class staterooms; and third class accommodation.

The *Carmania*'s turbine engines were superior to most others, helping the ship to make 20 knots on its trial trip, with a complete absence of the vibration usually associated with ships of this type.

Cross section of the *Carmania*.

The turbine engines of the *Carmania*.

On its maiden voyage in December 1905, the *Carmania* travelled from Liverpool to New York in 7 days, 9 hours, 31 minutes, averaging 15.97 knots over 2,835 miles. It continued to travel the Liverpool-New York route until 1910, carrying many famous passengers, including author H.G. Wells.

With the outbreak of the First World War in 1914, the *Carmania* was turned into an armed military cruiser, equipped with 4.7-inch guns. She sank a German cruiser during the Battle of Trindade. After repairs to extensive damage caused in the battle, the *Carmania* was used to patrol the Portuguese coast and Atlantic islands; assisted in the war's Gallipoli campaign; and was turned into a troopship. With the end of the First World War, the *Carmania* returned to passenger service until being scrapped in 1932.

Giant of the lake

Giant ships have not always been of the ocean-going variety. In 1906, a river steamer, built to operate on the Hudson in America, was proclaimed as the most magnificent lake boat ever built. It was 400 feet long, capable of 20 miles per hour from its 7,000-horsepower engines turning huge paddle wheels and had a passenger capacity of 4,500 travelling in parlour staterooms, each with its own deck veranda. It featured a double hull that needed 4 million pounds of steel and 700,000 rivets. To furnish the huge vessel, 1.6 million feet of oak, pine and mahogany was needed,

The giant river steamer that travelled the river Hudson.

with joiners using 3,400 pounds of nails. Two and half miles of steam pipes were laid, along with 1,600 electric lights. Wireless telegraph was available for passengers. Lifts between decks and open fireplaces in the passenger suits were also provided.

One of the boat's most interesting features was the steady tanks that held 100 tons of water used for ballast to prevent rocking and pitching. It was a system taken from battleships where water ballast was used to hold the vessels steady while heavy guns were fired.

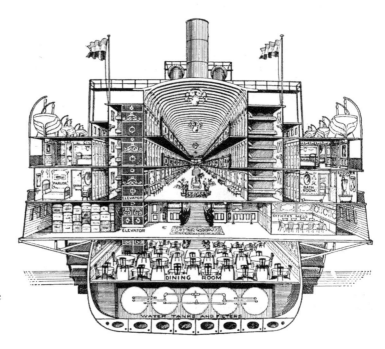

Cross section of the huge
river boat.

Electric Submarines

The first person to visualise the possibility of a boat that travelled under, rather than over, the water is generally reputed to be artist, sculptor, mathematician and sometime engineer Leonardo Da Vinci. In the sixteenth century he showed designs for a vessel that could travel beneath the surface of the sea for use in warfare to sink the ships above. His plans never went into production. Later, and still in the sixteenth century, amateur scientist William Bourne suggested a way of making a boat capable of travelling under water by use of expanding and contracting chambers to decrease the volume of a vessel to make it sink, and then to increase the volume, causing it to rise again.

What has come to be recognised as the first true submarine was the brainchild of Dutch innovator Cornelis Drebbel in 1623. That one was little more than an enclosed rowing boat powered by twelve oarsmen on a voyage 15 feet below the surface of the river Thames in London. Other ideas, not all of which saw reality, came from numerous English, French, German and American inventors over the coming years.

Among those who succeeded in building a working submersible craft was the American David Bushnell who, along with his brother Ezra, launched a kind of submarine called the Turtle, named after its similarity to two turtle shells placed together. It was made of oak and moved through the water by means of a propeller on the front operated by a hand crank and treadle from inside. Flooding and emptying an airtight chamber with water made it heavier or lighter, allowing it to submerge or rise in the water. A vertical propeller on the top of the machine helped it to ascend. The Turtle was designed mainly as a war machine to deliver an

Cross section of Bushnell's Turtle submarine.

underwater bomb to the bottom of the hull of an enemy ship. The problem was that the bomb could not be primed to explode when the craft was under water. So a clockwork timing mechanism was bult in for the detonation, with its timer set in advance of the Turtle actually diving. The operator therefore had to activate the timer before diving, pilot it to the enemy ship under water, disengage the bomb and then retreat before the timer detonated the explosion. In a trial run in 1776, Bushnell took the submersible down with the timer ticking but failed to find his target in time before the bomb exploded. Miraculously, he escaped.

With the advent of steam power in the nineteenth century, Swedish inventor Thorsten Nordenfeldt built a submarine driven by steam when it was on the surface which was shut down when the vessel submerged.

By the end of the nineteenth century, numerous designs had come and gone. Among them were plans from: Prussian army colonel Wilhelm Bauer for a sheet iron submarine powered by a two-man treadmill; American shoemaker Lodner D. Phillips for a hand-cranked, one-man submarine; Wilhelm Bauer for a sixteen-man vessel; French engineer Brutus de Villeroi for a vessel, 46 feet long, propelled by sixteen oarsmen and a 3-foot diameter hand-cranked propeller … and more.

But of all the forms of propulsion, from manpower to steam power, the strangest, and potentially the most dangerous, came with submarines powered by electricity – not the best of bedfellows when mixed with water.

The *Goubet I*

Claude Goubet was born in Lyon in 1837. As an inventor he filed a great many patents in the field of mechanics before getting interested in submarine design in 1880 and looking at actual construction in 1881. Four years later, he filed a patent for the first electric submarine, which he called the *Goubet I*. It was launched in 1887.

The *Goubet I* was cigar-shaped with a raised dome in the centre through which the two-man crew entered and which was then hermetically sealed with a cap. The two men sat on seats, back to back, with their heads in the dome. Small glass peepholes, which allowed them to see out, could be quickly sealed with caps if the glass was accidentally broken.

In the base of the vessel there were watertight chambers. When water was allowed into either or both of these chambers, the submarine sank. When a motor was used to pump the water out again, it rose to the surface.

Above the tanks and below the seats on which the sailors sat, there was a chamber full of compressed air equipped with pipes that led to the top of the dome, where they discharged air to the crew close to their faces. Stale air was evacuated by an air pump.

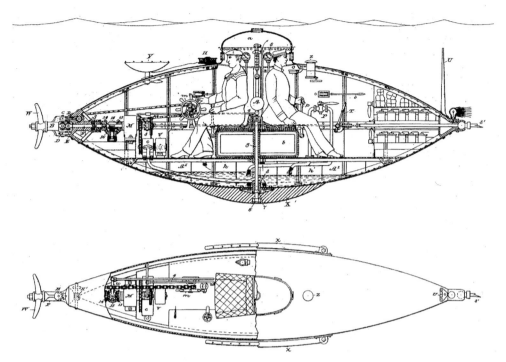

From the patent application, Goubet's electric submarine in profile and from above.

A motor, connected to a drive shaft, was used to drive the propeller and so move the vessel through the water. Alternatively, one of the two-man crew, sitting in extremely cramped conditions, was able to turn a crank to rotate the propeller. The propeller could be angled left and right to steer the vessel without the use of a rudder. A third method of propulsion came from oars that passed from the inside to the outside through watertight apertures.

To keep the submarine level in the water, a swinging pendulum was connected to pumps that drove water into tanks at the front or back of the vessel, depending on its angle in the water. If the submarine tilted backwards or forwards, the pendulum compensated to activate the appropriate pump, the weight of water pumped into the tanks quickly stabilising the angle of the vessel. The motor that drove the propeller, water pumps and air pumps was electric, powered by accumulators stored in lockers at the front of the vessel.

The *Goubet I* was also equipped with an electrically exploding torpedo, so that the submarine might be used to attack enemy ships. According to Goubet's patent, the torpedo was attached to the back of the submarine's dome by means of a fastening that could be operated from the inside. A long wire ran from the torpedo and onto a drum. For the purposes of attack, one of the crew sighted and lined the submarine up with the enemy ship before submerging, noting the bearing on a compass. The vessel was then submerged and, using the compass bearing, headed for the target.

Launching the *Goubet I*.

Once it reached the enemy ship, a crew member caused the submarine to submerge to a depth that took it under the ship. When it was in place, the torpedo was released to rise in the water and fix itself to the underside of the hull above.

The submarine then moved away, paying out the wire from the drum to the torpedo as it went. The number of revolutions of the drum indicated to the submarine crew the distance that they had moved. When the submarine had positioned itself at a safe enough distance, one crew member closed an electric circuit inside the dome that sent an electrical charge along the wire to fire the torpedo.

The *Goubet II*

Initially, as the *Goubet I* was tested and demonstrated, the French naval and military authorities took a keen interest. However, *Goubet I* was rejected as being too small and Goubet was invited to submit a design for something lager. The new vessel was called the *Goubet II*, and that also was powered by electricity, by this time with a more powerful motor. Three fins were added to improve stability and the vessel had provision for an extra torpedo. Despite the improvements and with problems from backers, the *Goubet II* suffered the same fate as the *Goubet I*. The inventor was ruined and died in 1903.

The *Gymnote*

The failure of the *Goubet II* did not turn the French authorities completely against the idea of electric submarines, and soon the attention was on another, this time called the *Gymnote*, launched in 1888.

The *Gymnote* was based on experiments by French naval architect Stanislas Charles Henri Dupuy de Lôme, who died in 1885, after which his work was carried on by marine engineer Gustave Zédé and automotive engineering pioneer Arthur Krebs. Together, the latter two engineers designed a submarine that was more practical than Goubet's vessels. The *Gymnote* was fitted with the first naval periscope and the first naval electrical gyrocompass.

Arthur Krebbs designed the electric motor that powered the submarine. The motor was connected directly to the vessel's propeller, which was capable of rotating at 250 revolutions per minute. The batteries to power the motor were in the bow of the submarine, arranged in six banks of cells. In this way the motor developed a maximum of 55 horsepower at 200 volts. The speed with which the motor turned and therefore the submarine travelled was controlled by the number of batteries used and the ways they were connected to vary the voltage, either in series (positive pole on one battery to negative pole on the next) or parallel (positive to positive and negative to negative).

The hull of the *Gymnote* was made of steel, supported by thirty-one circular frames. Three ballast tanks in the front, centre and rear were filled with water or emptied by electric or compressed air pumps, in order to control the sinking and rising of the vessel. Although it was the first to use a periscope, the device was soon abandoned due to difficulties with raising and lowering it and inefficient water seals that led to serious flooding on at least one occasion.

The *Gymnote* made about 2,000 dives during nearly twenty years of service in the French Navy until 1907, when it ran aground and was seriously damaged. Abandoned in dry dock, a valve was accidentally left open and the *Gymnote* flooded. Repairs were considered to be impractical and it was eventually sold for scrap in 1911. It is the *Gymnote*, rather than the *Goubet I* or *II*, which is more often remembered as history's first successful electric submarine.

The *Gymnote*, another successful French electric submarine.

Snow and Ice Boats

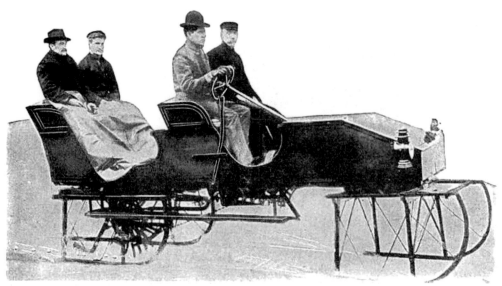

Petrol-driven sleigh for use on ice.

The road has not always been the only place for petrol-driven vehicles. Petrol engines were also used to power other devices, including boats like sleighs, designed for fast travel over ice. One such four-seater incorporated an engine that drove a spiked wheel between the back runners which dug into the ice and propelled the sleigh forwards. The direction of travel was controlled via a steering wheel that manoeuvred the sleigh's front runners.

In 1912, a Berlin auto show had on display a motor sleigh, in which a centrally mounted automobile engine drove a huge propeller at the rear. The vehicle was mounted on sledge-like runners along the length of the body to propel the vehicle across ice. At the rear of the vehicle two metal arms trailed above the ice and were connected to levers on either side of the body, where they could be manipulated by either the driver or passenger. Pulling the levers dug the metal arms into the ice to act as brakes. A separate set of movable runners at the front of the vehicle were connected to an automobile-type steering wheel to control direction.

To get round the problems of the difficulty of driving a car in deep snow, an American inventor in 1915 came up with a vehicle that ran on sledge-like runners instead of wheels. It was driven by a rear-mounted propeller with the front runners

Four more vehicles for driving across snow or ice, each one driven by a rear-mounted propeller.

being steerable by a normal car's steering wheel. A 14-foot long prototype fitted with a 60-horsepower rear-mounted engine attained speeds of 35 miles per hour. In looks, the so-called aero-sleigh appeared to be the kind of vehicle that would be driven across a frozen lake, but it was designed also to be driven on snowy roads and was said to be as manoeuvrable as a normal motor car. The proposal was to fit the prototype

Streamlining helped this ice vehicle to attain claimed speeds of up to 150 miles per hour.

design with a limousine body and to establish a sledge-bus line in the suburbs of Chicago by 1916. There is no evidence to suggest the plan came to fruition.

A huge rear-mounted propeller drove an ice touring car-cum-boat also built in 1915. At 22 feet long and 8 feet wide it was cable of carrying eight passengers at speeds of up to 50 miles per hour. The vehicle sped over ice on runners front and rear, with the front runners connected to the body by vertical spindles that allowed them to turn in response to an ordinary motor vehicle type of steering wheel in the front of the craft's body. Iceboats on sledge-like runners and driven by rear-mounted propellers were also popular around this time in northern countries like Finland.

An American ice yacht, capable of speeds of up to 100 miles per hour.

In 1920, two American aeronautical engineers built an aero ice yacht with a 100-horsepower engine that drove a rear-mounted propeller to achieve speeds of 150 miles per hour over ice. The body was designed to accommodate twelve passengers. With a little extra fine-tuning and streamlining the inventors claimed to be confident their ice yacht would be capable of 175 miles per hour.

Yet another propeller-driven motor sleigh constructed by an American enthusiast in 1928 was said to be capable of speeds of 150 miles per hour. Its speed was attributed to a streamlined design culminating in a pointed nose with a single blade beneath. Two blades were also situated on fins at the back of the vehicle. Fifteen feet long, it carried six passengers in upholstered seats. To stop the craft, the driver pulled a lever which pushed a cast-iron spiked shoe into the ice.

Running on either road wheels or ice runners, an American sightseeing craft from 1922 that carried ten passengers.

More Strange Craft

Here's a look at some of the many other types of water-based craft, some of which enjoyed more success than others – and some of which never got beyond the dreams of ambitious designers who failed to understand the true practicality of their ideas.

Amphibious autos

In 1905 reports from America detailed a craft that looked like a small rowing boat without oars but with wheels. It was designed to travel on water and ice, or even over land. A petrol engine powered two large wheels at the rear and a single wheel at the front was used for steering. When the craft left the land, it floated like a normal boat while hinged paddles attached to the rear wheels drove it through the water. When the water iced over, spikes were attached to the rear wheels, a single runner was fitted under the front wheel and two further runners were placed beneath the craft between the driving wheels. It was said that any of these modifications could be made in minutes.

Three-wheeled vehicle for travelling over land, water or ice.

Amphibious auto on water from French inventor Jules Reveillier.

Another similar vehicle, still taking the basic shape of a boat, was equipped with four wheels for land and a rear propeller for use in water, with the power shifting from one to the other by means of a simple lever. Demonstrated by its French inventor Jules Reveillier, it attained speeds of 20 miles per hour on land and 9 miles per hour on water.

A third design of amphibious auto came from a retired rear admiral in the United States Navy. This one, known as a pleasure surf boat, had two 4-foot diameter wheels at the font and a third at the back, plus a propeller whose blades measured nearly 2 feet across. The rear wheel was mounted within a tailpiece pivoted to the hull of the craft and operated by a tiller in the cockpit, to steer the vehicle on land or in the sea.

In 1915, when cars were driven onto ferries for a short trip across a bay in Washington, the paddles that moved the ferry through the water were driven by the car it carried. The car was driven onto the ferry, a jack was used to lift the back wheels a few inches off the deck, then a wooden wheel attached to the paddles on each side of the raft was fixed to the spokes of the car wheel using leather clamps. The car driver then did everything he would normally do when driving along a road. The back wheels, however, no longer in contact with a solid surface, revolved

A ferry boat powered by the car that it was carrying.

freely and drove the paddles of the ferry. An average lightweight car could drive the ferry at about 8 miles an hour.

An auto boat from 1921 and built in Europe used wheels with tyres on the rims and paddles on their inner surfaces. In this way, the same wheels were used to drive it along the road or through the water. The body resembled the hull of a boat, with one large wheel in front surrounded by a rudder-like shield as the wheel was used to steer on land or water.

A French land and water ship which also made its debut in 1921 began life as a military tank before becoming a passenger-carrying vehicle. On land it was propelled by endless treadwheels like a tank. In water it travelled like a launch. The strangely shaped machine was successfully tested in the port of Marseilles, where it carried six passengers over land and water.

News stories of land and water vehicles of this time reported that their commercial value appeared to be doubtful.

A European auto boat from the 1920s.

Half tank, half passenger-carrying craft for use on land or water.

This sporty water and land craft was reputed to attain speeds of up to 40 miles per hour once out of the water and on a good road.

Cycle boats

A craze for cycle boats in the 1900s was epitomised by one built by a New York carpenter in 1907. It was 8 feet long, 5 feet wide and weighed 60 pounds, taking the form of a typical bicycle frame with twin floats substituted for the back wheel and a single float in place of the front wheel. Sitting on a normal bicycle saddle the rider peddled the craft to drive a propeller at the back. Provision was also made for the addition of a sail, carried in a tube attached to the frame. The addition of a small petrol motor was also suggested to turn machines of this type into motorcycle boats.

A machine to be used either for leisure or for life-saving when a swimmer got into difficulties was designed by an American inventor. Its frame was made of aluminium tubing with two air-inflated tubes attached for buoyancy. The swimmer

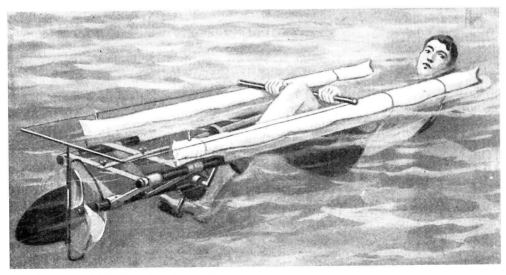

A cycleboat, useful for the swimming cyclist.

The following text appears within the illustration:

A Canoe Propelled by Hand-Operated Cranks Made Fair Speed

This Craft with Rotating Floats could Also be Driven by an Air Propeller

THE craze for watercycling has struck Paris this year with great force. Recently the first annual watercycle race meet was held on a lake in one of the Paris parks. Many odd and curious craft with almost as many different means of propulsion, were entered in the various events. As these photographs of eleven of the most novel of the watercycles show, there were air propellers, water-screw propellers and paddle-wheels, driven both by hand and by foot power, among them. The air-propelled devices raced in a class by themselves.

Odd-Shaped Floats, Like the Pontoons of a Flying Boat

A Comfortable Two-Passenger Craft with the Propelling Machinery Less Conspicuous than Most

This Machine Won Second Prize in the Air-Propelled Class

Winner of the Race for Cycles Driven by Water Propellers

The Winner of the Race for Air-Propelled Watercycles was This Simple Machine

The Only Woman Contestant Caused a Sensation But did Not Win a Prize

A Machine with Cylindrical Floats That Made Good Speed

Like Many Other Contestants, This One Has a Bicycle Frame as the Basis of Its Mechanism

This Watercycle, with a Stern Paddle Wheel Like a Mississippi Steamboat, Showed Great Tractive Power

The French watercycle race meeting as illustrated in a 1914 issue of *Popular Mechanics* magazine.

or driver lay back in a harness and used peddles like those of a bicycle to turn a propeller while a handlebar was used to rotate a rudder for steering. The machine was adjustable according to the height of driver and could be folded for storage and portability.

The interest in bicycle boats continued into the next decade. In 1914, the first annual watercycle race meeting was held on a lake in a Paris park. Various events saw the appearance of many different types of machine, some with propellers under water, others with air propellers in the air above the water, some with inflatable wheels, others with hand or foot-driven paddles, some resembling canoes, others taking the shape of giant skis.

In September that year, *Popular Mechanics* magazine carried two pages on the many splendid designs of bicycle boats popular in France at that time.

Canoe sidecar

A motorcycle sidecar made in the shape of a canoe was seen at a London motoring exhibition in 1925. The 14-foot craft was held in place on the motorcycle by a series of straps that could be quicky unfastened for launching into water in a matter

A motorcycle sidecar that converted to a canoe.

of seconds. Back on the side of the motorcycle after a trip across the water, the canoe was used as a sidecar for one or two passengers. Despite its size it was said not to interfere with the handling of the motorcycle.

Cross-Atlantic boat

In 1927, two intrepid English adventurers planned to cross the Atlantic in a 12-foot boat with no engine, oars, steam power or even a sail. In its place, the small craft had a windmill at the front geared to a propeller at the rear to drive the boat forwards. The trip was expected to take fifty days, but there is no evidence to suggest it ever took place.

The small craft with no engine or sails in which it was hoped to cross the Atlantic.

Flying boats

Inventors of the 1920s and 1930s were often keen to merge two or more modes of transport into one vehicle. A flying boat designed in the 1930s combined the features of an amphibian, dirigible gyrocopter and an ordinary aeroplane. The craft had a single wing that was actually more like a rotating disc filled with gas or hot air and mounted above the cabin. This and a propeller at the rear were driven by a petrol engine in the centre of the body, with space for passengers and crew on each side. With retractable wheels the craft could be landed on land or water. The rotating disc added to the lift needed to get the machine into the

Had plans come to fruition, this strange craft would have combined a boat with a dirigible, gyrocopter and aeroplane.

air, but also acted as a parachute on its descent. Two models were built and flown although there is no evidence that a full-size craft ever made it into service.

Hydroplanes

The design of the hydroplane meant that rather than floating on water, it skimmed above the surface on a cushion of air. One such, made in 1915, used forward-facing funnels that gathered air as it travelled at speed and discharged it under the hull to produce the air cushion. The motive power was a large propeller on an elevated mast at the rear of the craft.

Another, produced in the early 1920s, used a curve-shaped hull and was again driven by rear propellers. This one, known as a hydroglider, sported an exceptionally luxurious enclosed cabin to accommodate passengers with an open-air cockpit for the driver in front.

When a speedboat is travelling fast, its prow tends to lift clear of the water. So why not attach a pair of wings and take it even higher? That was the thinking that led two American inventors to produce a special kind of hydroplane that they called a waterboat in 1930. Designed for sport and recreation rather than a means of real transport, the craft was capable of lifting the prow where the rider sat 10 feet into the air with an outboard motor as the driving force attached to the stern still in the

A 1915 hydroplane (top) and hydroglider from the 1920s.

The waterboat takes to the air.

water. The rider held a joystick which controlled the elevation while the rudder was operated by foot controls. The craft needed about 25 feet of water before take-off was achieved and travelled at speeds of up to 50 miles per hour.

Trains on boats

A car ferry operating across the Baltic Sea in the 1920s was equipped with railway lines to link with those on land. As the ferry docked, the bow opened like a pair of giant jaws. A whole train, comprising twenty passengers and forty-eight freight cars, could be driven into the ship's hold. When the jaws were closed, the bow of the ship was designed to plough through the water in the usual way or even crush ice that might be encountered on the trip, which linked Berlin to Copenhagen via the port of Warnemünde in Germany.

Taking trains across the sea, on railway lines inside a ferry.

Mortorised surfboard

Outboard racing was a popular pastime in the 1930s. The contestants drove small hydroplanes, designed to skim across the surface of the water at high speeds with the capability of performing tight turns. Mostly the boats were of a conventional design, but occasionally a far more radical design came to the fore.

Seen in a 1936 race was a hydrofoil boat that was little more than a surfboard with an engine mounted on the back but with winglike projections known as sponsons sprouting from each side. They consisted of cigar-shaped cylinders attached to the tip of each 'wing'. When the craft was at rest these lay on the surface of the water to balance and keep the boat afloat. As it took off at speed, the sponsons lifted

Hydrofoil boat seen at a 1936 race meeting.

away from the water so that the craft was racing purely on its hull. When it came to turning the craft, the hull lifted from the water at an angle and one of the sponsons dipped into the water to maintain stability. An outboard race was often won or lost by the way a driver executed tight turns, and this design helped to achieve such turns with more speed than usual.

Part IV

Travel by Air

Following the first manned flight in 1903, aircraft design and manufacture took off and moved fast. For a while it seemed the airship would lead the way, but after a series of fatal crashes that demonstrated in the most dramatic fashion the true danger of travelling in a cabin beneath a balloon filled with gas, more conventional aircraft took over and the era of aviation blossomed. Many sowed the seeds of ideas and designs that developed into the aircraft we see today. Not surprisingly, however, there were a lot more designs that fell by wayside, which, while seeming to be practical at the time, can now be viewed as more of the weird and wonderful means of transport from the past.

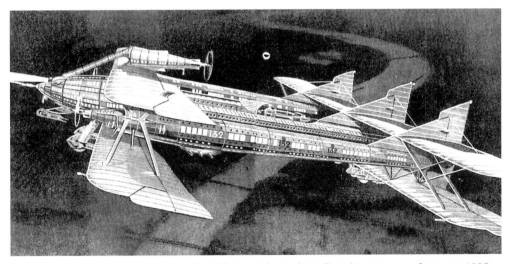

How aircraft of the future might have looked, as prophesised at a British aviation conference in 1925.

Aviation for all, as advertised in the 1920s.

The Age of the Airship

Before the aeroplane, it must have seemed obvious to aviation enthusiasts that the only way to get off the ground must be in a machine or other kind of contraption that was lighter than air. Since no machine, nor its pilot, could fulfil that need, a means was needed to attach a heavier-than-air device to a balloon of some kind filled with enough lighter-than-air gas to lift man and machine.

It began in 1783 with the invention of the hot-air balloon in France and it wasn't long before inventors began to look at the possibility of balloons that did more than simply go up and down and drift on the wind. French engineer Jean Baptiste Meusnier designed an elongated balloon driven forwards by propellers and with a basket below attached by ropes to carry passengers, although there is no evidence that his design ever saw reality.

Much the same can be said for a rather fanciful drawing that appeared in *The Graphic*, a British weekly illustrated newspaper, in 1877. The illustration, with no

A rather fanciful idea for getting off the ground, as depicted in *The Graphic* newspaper in 1877.

A 1925 artist's impression of what the future might look like, when airships over our cities would be as common as trains and steamships.

further explanation and simply titled 'A suggestion for a flying machine', showed a man high above the ground suspended from voluminous parachute-like wings with ropes attached apparently for steering purposes and which were supported in turn by large spherical balloons, presumably filled with a lighter-than-air gas.

Equally strange was a patent granted in 1887 to French inventor Charles Wulff who came up with the idea of propelling and steering an airship by harnessing birds such as eagles, vultures or condors to the top of his apparatus. This strangely designed contraption consisted of a balloon filled with gas and a cradle below it to hold the aeronaut. Above the balloon stood a platform to which the birds were harnessed and with space for the pilot. Above that a parachute-like arrangement was erected to help regulate the balloon's descent. The aeronaut below and the pilot above communicated via a speaking tube. The flight of the birds, harnessed to prevent them escaping but free to flap their wings, was utilised to make the machine move in any desired direction that included forwards, backwards, left and right, or even for ascending and descending. All it needed was for the birds to flap their wings in the way they would naturally when flying free. By movement of the harnesses, the direction of their constricted flight was controlled by the pilot independent of their own will.

There is no evidence to suggest that Monsieur Wulff's apparatus ever got off the ground. By this time, however, far more practical methods of building and flying airships had already begun to emerge.

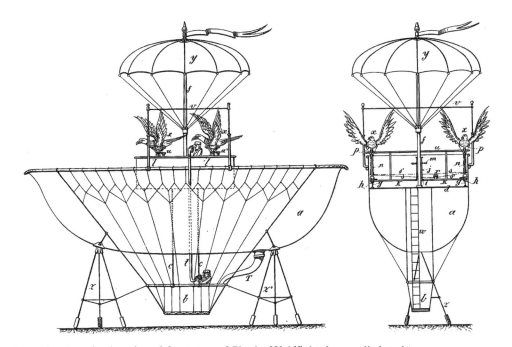

Patent drawings for the side and front view of Charles Wulff's bird-controlled airship.

Early attempts

Practical designs for working airships began in earnest in the 1850s. The first passenger-carrying craft came from French engineer Henri Giffard who, in 1852, designed and built a steam-powered airship which he called a dirigible. The elongated balloon that lifted the craft was 144 feet long and filled with hydrogen. The steam engine that powered it weighed 350 pounds and developed 3 horsepower to turn a large propeller at 110 revolutions per minute. On its maiden voyage it flew 20 miles at a speed of 6 miles per hour.

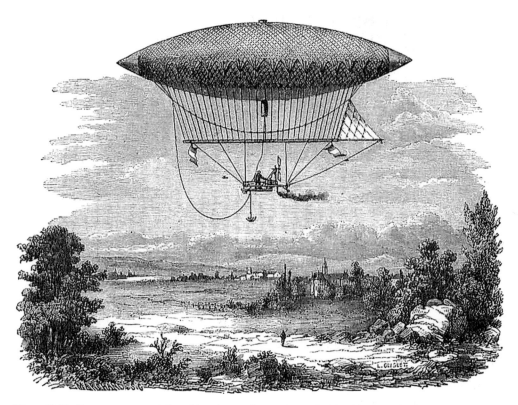

Henri Giffard's steam-powered dirigible takes to the air above the French countryside.

In 1876, American inventor Charles Ritchel demonstrated his own form of airship that used a cylindrical bag of lighter-than-air gas to lift it off the ground. The gas bag was attached to a brass frame beneath which the pilot sat, turning a crank that operated a propeller at the front of the frame to drive the machine forwards. Ritchel flew his craft inside an exhibition hall at Philadelphia's Centennial Exposition, and he continued to demonstrate short but moderately successful flights over the next two years.

Charles Ritchel's one-man airship lifted into the air by a cylindrical bag of gas.

The Zeppelin

Airship design rapidly improved throughout the late nineteenth century until it reached a peak with the launch of the Zeppelin in 1895, named after its inventor Count Ferdinand von Zeppelin. From the start, the Zeppelin featured twin 15-horsepower engines, flew at speeds of up to 25 miles per hour and carried compartments beneath the hydrogen-filled balloon for crew and passengers.

In May 1909, a Zeppelin took off and covered a distance of 850 miles in thirty-seven hours, a journey that could easily have taken it from somewhere like Cologne in Germany to London and back again. The news of this event worried anyone who cared about what arial supremacy might mean to a nation in the event of war. It particularly worried the English, many of whom were suspicious of German motives. That said, the Zeppelin didn't complete its epic journey unscathed. The airship collided with a tree and was badly damaged during the latter part of its flight. However, the damage proved to be repairable on the spot and the airship completed its journey. Compared to earlier attempts at building airships, this in itself

The USS *Los Angeles*, an American Navy airship designated as ZR-3 and built by the German Zeppelin works in 1923–24.

proved the superiority of the Zeppelin, the design of which was being continually improved. By the time of that mammoth 850-mile journey, the Zeppelin comprised seventeen separate gas bags or balloons inside its huge envelope, each of which was separated from its neighbour by sheet aluminium partitions. The bursting of any one of these gas bags would have had no effect on the others.

The *Deutchland*, one of a fleet of Zeppelins that was set to become a passenger-carrying service operating in Germany around 1909.

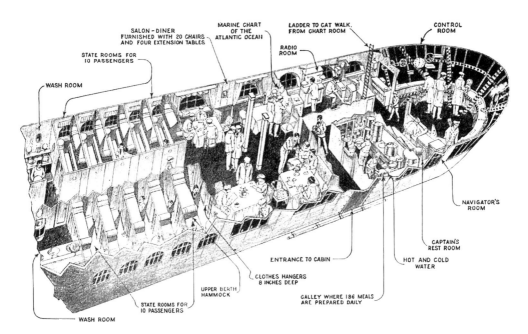

An artist's impression of the luxurious interior of a Zeppelin airship.

The Zeppelin and the way it evolved proved to be one of the greatest ever airship designs and Zeppelins continued to fly well into the twentieth century. The *Graf* Zeppelin of 1928 was one of the most famous versions. It achieved many transatlantic crossings and, by the time it was finally decommissioned in 1937, had made 590 flights, of which 144 were ocean crossings.

A rowing airship

In America in 1905, inventor Alva L. Reynolds unveiled his aerial rowing boat, which he called a Man-Angel, named after the city of Los Angeles in which he lived. The gas bag that lifted his craft into the air was shaped like a long cylinder, blunt at one end and pointed at the other. Beneath this, the inventor sat in a cradle holding a pair of oars, similar to those in a rowing boat, but culminating in large paddles. Using these, the pilot simply rowed the craft through the air, as he attempted to reproduce the motions of a bird's wing. The inventor claimed that this meant his airship needed less gas than most and that he was working towards the elimination of a gas bag altogether, relying on the rowing motion of his paddle-wings to propel the craft into and through the air. There is no evidence to suggest this ever happened.

The early years of the twentieth century saw airship design and construction forge ahead, with advertisements even beginning to appear in popular magazines

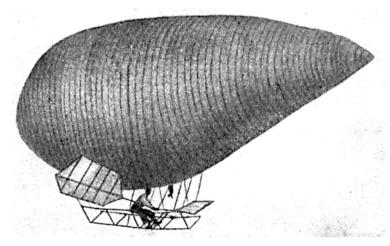

The aerial rowing boat in action.

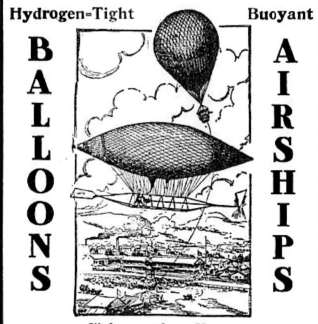

A 1907 advertisement for popularising airships.

aimed at any person who might like to buy one for their use. All sizes from the smallest models to the largest capable of long voyages were available, with buyers assured that their purchases would be hydrogen-tight and buoyant.

A radical new design

In 1902 American inventor Charles Tolliver suggested an airship in which passengers would travel inside the gas bag, rather than in a gondola beneath. His airship's 250-foot long silk gas bag was stretched over an aluminium frame 40 feet wide and 44 feet high, but the hydrogen gas pumped into the bag didn't fill the entire space. Areas were left empty at each end, connected by a passageway along the bottom of the bag. Above this passage three more compartments were provided, one for passengers and crew, the other two for four engines, each of which required its own engineer. The cabins were protected from the gas inside the balloon by double layers of silk over aluminium wire walls. Passenger cabin floors were made of bamboo strips laced together. The engines drove propellers at each end of the bag. A pilot at the front of the craft directed the movements of the ship and was in communication with his crew by telephone.

Unlike other airships, Tolliver's invention had no need of a steering rudder because the propellers were mounted on flexible shafts that allowed them to be angled in different directions, thus steering the craft through the air. The rotation of the blades of the front and back propellers could be reversed to enable the airship to travel forwards or backwards.

In 1907, after five years of work on the airship, Tolliver announced it was ready to be launched in San Diego, where it was built. A series of accidents, however, prevented the launch. Four more years of work followed before Tolliver again announced that his airship was ready for launching in 1911. But despite the engines being fired up, it failed to rise into the air. Financial problems followed, with investors backing out and then the City Health Department declared the

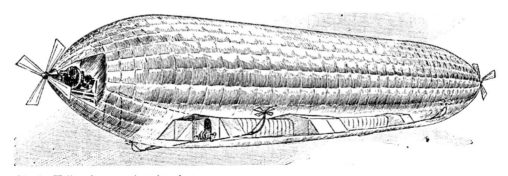

Charles Tolliver's unusual airship design.

With a dirigible moored to the top of a mast, passengers might disembark and descend to the ground by lift.

For transatlantic airship voyagers, it was suggested that a battleship might serve as a supply station mid-ocean.

hydrogen gas in the airship's bag had become explosive and dangerous. Tolliver was ordered to deflate the airship, but the weather did the job for him. On the night of 20 December 1911, a storm hit the area and high winds ripped Tolliver's airship to pieces.

The final chapter of the story was even more dramatic. One night in May 1912, as Tolliver and his wife were returning to their home, the couple were shot and stabbed by their secretary and chauffeur, Herbert Lewis, who was also an investor in Tolliver's company. Lewis stood trial for the murders but was found not guilty by reason of insanity.

The end of an era

Airship design culminated in the arrival of the *Hindenburg*, another version of the Zeppelin, which carried the more conventional gondola beneath the gas bag. The passenger quarters of this huge craft must have appeared minute compared to the size of the balloon required to lift it, but even so, they were well-appointed with thirty-four cabins capable of carrying seventy-two passengers. Lavish dining rooms, lounges, a writing room, smoking room, bar and promenades where passengers

The luxurious *Hindenburg* airship moored before take-off.

could take in the spectacular views below were all incorporated. In 1936, it flew more than 1,000 passengers on ten round trips between Germany and America. It must have seemed like the era of luxurious airship travel had arrived. And then disaster struck.

Six years before, in 1930, the R101, a British airship, had crashed in France and the fire that resulted from the crash killed forty-six passengers and crew. Then, in

The British R101 airship.

The *Hindenburg* disaster of 1937, which put an end to the dream of passenger-carrying airships.

May 1937, the LZ 129 *Hindenburg*, the world's largest passenger airship, exploded and crashed in New Jersey, killing thirty-six passengers and crew. Although airships were still utilised by the military for many years to come, the *Hindenburg* crash and other notable airship fires and accidents were largely responsible for ending the age of the airship as civilian passenger-carrying craft.

The Ups and Downs of Early Flight

Airships made manned flight possible, but they were almost ridiculously inefficient when it came to the comparatively tiny size of the compartments in which passengers and crew travelled against the immense size of the balloon or gas bag needed to get them airborne. They were also prone to bursting into flames. If manned flight was to progress at the end of the nineteenth century it must have seemed clear that lighter-than-air machines were not the way forward. Inventors needed to find a way to get heavier-than-air machines off the ground.

That once seemingly impossible feat was eventually accomplished by American inventors and aviation pioneers Orville and Wilbur Wright. Their flying machine was called *The Flyer*. It was made of spruce and ash wood, with the frame covered in cotton cloth. Metal fittings were made from mild steel, with the engine block cast from an alloy of aluminium and copper. It was a biplane with wings above and below the space where the pilot lay in the centre of the lower wing. The wingspan was 40 feet. On 17 December 1903, *The Flyer* made four flights, the first lasting only twelve seconds and covering no more than 120 feet. The best flight of the day covered 842 feet in fifty-nine seconds.

The Wright brothers get the recognition for starting the aviation age, but before them there were a great many less well-known and now all but forgotten pioneers who tried and failed to get into the air with a succession of weird and wonderful flying machines. In the 1890s, plans were published to build a gyrocopter with

The Wright brothers' aeroplane, from an English patent drawing.

A cartoon of the day laughs at early aviation attempts.

two umbrella-like propellers arranged horizontally to whirl each side of the pilot to provide vertical lift. It was just one of the many ideas that failed to materialise. Others were more practical.

The Glider King

The earliest documented flights by heavier-than-air machines showed that manned flight was possible, but not if the plan was to start at ground level and take off into the air. The alternative was for the machine to start from an elevated position from

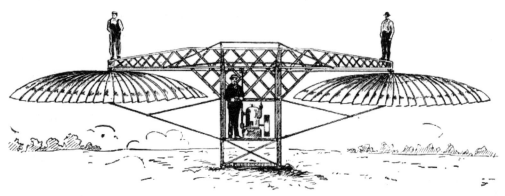

A gyrocopter that never got past the planning stage.

Early aviation pioneer Otto Lilienthal.

which it glided to earth. German aviation pioneer Otto Lilienthal was among early pioneers who saw the possibilities that came from manned gliders.

In 1894, Lilienthal built a machine in which the pilot was suspended from a bar beneath wide wings, not unlike a modern hang-glider. Using this, flights were made from both natural hills and one that Lilienthal had built for the purpose near Berlin. Direction of travel was controlled by the pilot shifting his weight from side to side. It was his various successes that earned Lilienthal the name of the Glider King.

The soaring machine

Prime among other important glider pioneers was Octave Chanute, a civil engineer who turned to studying aviation after he retired in 1883. Being too old to fly by this time, he teamed up with a couple of younger partners named Augustus Herring and William Avery. Together they built and tested a number of ideas for gliders, which led Chanute to at first believe that the way forward was with a glider that used twelve pivoting wings in two tiers of six.

When that failed to take off, Chanute and his partners began experimenting with a more conventional approach with a two-winged glider based on an improved version of Lilienthal's original design. In his patent of 1897, Chanute described his device as a soaring machine, explaining that its purpose was to imitate the soaring of birds, which is accomplished while the wings are held still rather than flapping.

Chanute's improvement on Lilienthal's glider provided a stationary seat for the pilot with each wing pivoted in a way that allowed it to move backwards and forwards and so preserve the balance of both the machine and the pilot.

The likes of Lilienthal and Chanute went a long way towards showing that a man could sail through the air, but not that they could take off from the ground to do so. It wasn't long, however, before aviation engineers in Britain, France, Germany and

Octave Chanute's multi-winged glider.

America took up that challenge and, unsurprisingly perhaps, some of the early pioneers took inspiration from the way birds flew.

The *Artificial Albatross*

Jean Marie Le Bris was a sailor who took his inspiration for a flying machine from watching albatrosses in flight. So he killed one and examined its wings. The glider he built in 1856 was based on the scaled-up shape of an albatross. It had a 50-foot wingspan with hand-operated levers that changed the angles of the wings and foot-operated pedals that changed the position of the tail. He called his craft the *Artificial Albatross*.

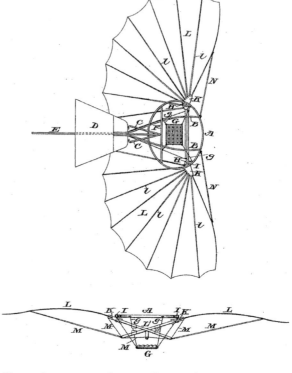

Chanute's soaring machine, as illustrated in its patent.

The *Artificial Albatross*, based on the way the birds fly.

The contraption was mounted onto a horse-drawn cart, which was driven along a road and into the wind with Le Bris on board. When he judged that sufficient speed had been reached, he untied the restraining ropes and, according to reports of the day, his machine rose about 300 feet into the air and made a short flight of about 600 feet.

Although the *Albatross* was still essentially a glider, it did have the distinction of starting from ground level and flying upwards, rather than starting at a high level and gliding down. Even so, a second attempt at flying the *Albatross* involved it being launched from a mast about 100 feet above the ground. That flight wasn't so successful. The machine hit the ground too hard and broke, badly injuring the pilot.

The *Aerial Steamer*

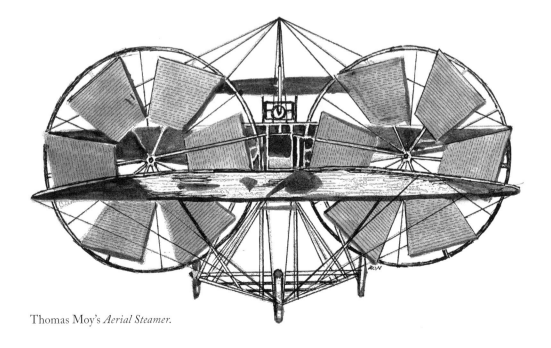

Thomas Moy's *Aerial Steamer*.

The late 1800s were still very much the age of steam, and in 1874 that's what was used to power English engineer Thomas Moy's *Aerial Steamer*.

The steam engine was fuelled by methylated spirits to drive two huge six-bladed propellers mounted between two wings made from linen stretched across bamboo frames. It was tested, unmanned but tethered, on a circular gravel track around a fountain in the grounds of the Crystal Palace in South London. On the first test run all it did was churn up the gravel. So wooden decking was laid over the gravel and a second attempt made.

Moy had calculated that his machine needed to reach 35 miles per hour to lift off, but it never exceeded a speed of 12 miles per hour and, according to Moy, never left the ground, although there were later reports that suggested that the *Aerial Seamer* managed to rise 6 inches into the air.

The sesquiplane

In France in 1883, French engineer Alexandre Goupil demonstrated a machine that took the form of a large rounded body housing a steam engine to drive a propeller at the front and with a rudder hanging from the back. A wing protruded from each side of the housing with a total wingspan across the two of nearly 20 feet. Below the housing a structure allowed a man to stand between two landing wheels, with his feet resting on peddles attached to the front wheel with a slightly smaller one at the rear. His machine was called the sesquiplane.

There's no evidence to suggest that the machine was ever tested with its steam engine, but an unpowered version was known to have lifted into the air with two men on board, in a wind of about 14 miles per hour.

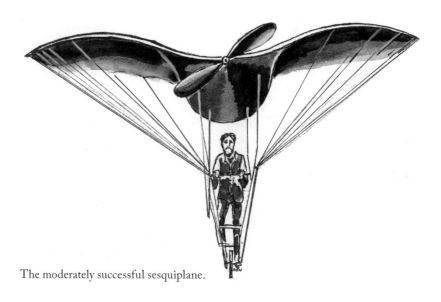

The moderately successful sesquiplane.

The bat planes

It wasn't just birds that inspired the design of early aircraft. Those built by French inventor Clement Ader were known to bear a resemblance to gigantic bats. He built two machines, called the *Ader Éole* and the *Ader Avion No.3*, its two predecessors having been damaged in trials and experiments. Both machines had wide wingspans and steam-driven propellers.

Later in life, many of Ader's somewhat exaggerated claims of manned flight were disproven, but it is pretty much accepted that, in 1890, he did manage to make a very short flight in the *Ader Éole*, which eventually earned him the title, among his fellow countrymen, of the Father of Aviation.

A gigantic biplane

In 1891, American-born but nationalised English inventor Hiram Maxim patented an enormous biplane, 145 feet long and with a wingspan of 105 feet, which supported two steam-driven propellers. Later, he added more wings. Because it was not easy to control and would be aerodynamically unstable, Maxim built his machine more for research purposes than for true flight. For that reason, it was made to run along railway-like tracks and restrained to prevent lift-off. Nevertheless, in 1894, it broke one of its retraining rails and did indeed lift off, becoming damaged in the process. Maxim then abandoned his experiments until later in the twentieth century, when he switched from steam to internal combustion engines for his experiments in manned flight.

All these usually unsuccessful, not to say dangerous, attempts at building flying machines were soon eclipsed by the Wright brothers, who began their experiments in manned flight with gliders, culminating in the legendary flight of *The Flyer* in 1903. After that, aviation history was changed forever.

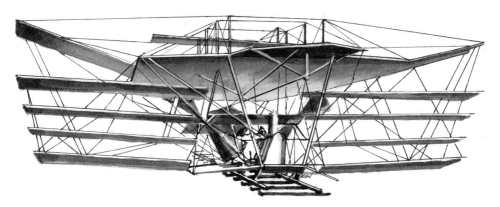

Hiram Maxim's enormous biplane.

The Shape of Planes to Come

In the early days, flying was a dangerous occupation.

In the early years of manned flight, futurists keenly discussed the pros and cons of two types of flying machine. The first relied on soaring flight, in which a small, lightweight motor might be used to drive propellers to lift the machine and then to allow it to rise as needed in the air, after which sustaining and propelling power relied on wind and gravity. The second was dynamic flight, which relied more on

Two designs from the early 1900s by French aviator Louis Paulhan: an unusual triplane (above) and his so-called Torpedo (below), which was reputed to have made several successful flights in 1912.

a much heavier engine to drive a propeller, or propellers, which kept the machine aloft. In the first type of craft, sufficient gliding capabilities allowed descent to earth in relative safely in the event of engine failure. On the other hand, designs that relied purely on the power of a heavy engine to keep the craft in the air meant that the entire machine would become unmanageable in the event of engine failure and would inevitably end in it falling to earth like a stone, to the detriment of both the pilot and those unfortunate enough to be on the ground below.

Meanwhile, fantasists indulged in all kinds of flying machines that they thought might soon become commonplace – like a flying motorcycle envisaged by an English motorcycling magazine.

Even more fanciful maybe was a pilot's outer garment that could be converted into a parachute. As the airman ejected from his aircraft in time of trouble, he activated the garment, which spread out around him like a nineteenth-century lady's hoop skirt, lowering him slowly and safely to earth. That was the theory, anyway. Evidence of its use and success is scant.

How an early twentieth-century motorcycling magazine saw the possibility of its readers taking to the air.

The strange sport of aero-skiing.

Slightly more practical, but no less frightening, was a craze that developed in Europe during the 1900s for aero-skiing. This involved a glider equipped with ski-like runners that was raced down a ski slope until sufficient speed was reached for the operator to manipulate a mechanism to elevate the rudder, at which point the glider left the ski slope and ascended, often very briefly, into the air.

Taking passengers

In January 1908, French aeronaut Henri Farman won a $10,000 prize for being the first to fly in a full circle, over a distance of about 0.6 miles. His aircraft flew at heights of between 25 and 35 feet at 24 miles per hour. The following year, Farman set a

A parachute that aviators might wear as an item of clothing.

world record for endurance with a flight of 145.59 miles. In 1912, he and his brother Maurice established an aeronautical factory for building Farman biplanes, which from the start were capable of carrying at least one passenger alongside the pilot.

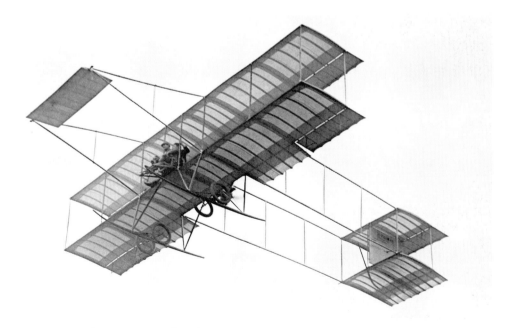

Farman's plane with a passenger on board.

The French Albessard and Russian Sikorsky planes were among those that looked at early attempts of adding a passenger compartment to an aeroplane. In the Sikorski plane sixteen passengers plus a pilot were carried for fifteen minutes. With only nine on board, it remained airborne for two hours six minutes.

In February 1911, French pioneer aviator Léon Lematin transported himself and seven passengers for the first time, with a combined weight of more than 74 stone. The flight only lasted five minutes, but it set a world record. The following month, Lematin made three more flights, each time with more passengers, until he reached thirteen.

Meanwhile, inventors and experimenters had been continuing to look at many different, often weird and wonderful, ways to fly, many of which in the early days were influenced by nature.

Flying like a bird …

In 1905 there were reports of several English scientists and at least one American building flying machines based on a study of the working of birds' wings. The English investigations showed that a bird's wing was so arranged that, during the upward movement of the wing there is the least resistance to the air and that air even passes through the wing. On the downward stroke of the wing, the opposite is

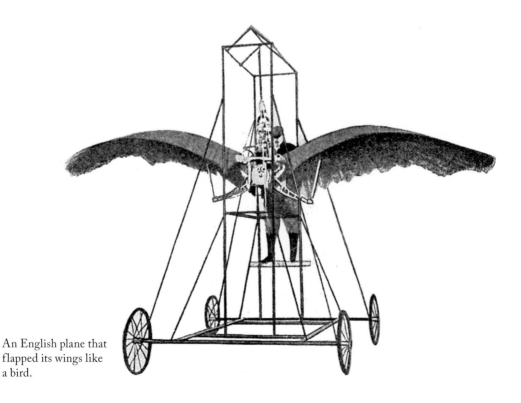

An English plane that flapped its wings like a bird.

true, as the feathers close to provide a lifting motion. It was only natural, then, that a craft should be designed using a gigantic pair of wings, measuring 20 feet from tip to tip and with a surface of 60 square feet. Their design was as close as possible to that of a crow's wing.

These mammoth wings were attached to a frame to carry the pilot and an engine to drive their flapping motion at 100 flaps per minute. The whole thing was mounted on four bicycle-type wheels. In trials, the machine managed to lift itself 2 feet off the ground.

The wings of this English machine were artificial, but in America an Ohio inventor tried something similar, using thousands of real turkey wing feathers. Launched by running the machine down a steep incline, its inventor claimed that it would need no engine, and that it would simply fly in the way a bird does. Further experiments by a professor at Los Angeles Polytechnic High School resulted in a similar machine with wings modelled after those of an eagle. They measured 27 feet from tip to tip.

… and an insect

A similar birdlike plane from America.

When it came to looking at nature for inspiration, early aviators didn't stop at birds.

A plane said to be influenced by the shape and aerodynamics of a dragonfly.

French inventor René Demanest's design was based on the shape of a dragonfly. It had two wings mounted on a long body and tail. Also unusual was the placing of the motor that drove the propeller above the wings. The pilot, more usually found on a framework beneath the wings, sat on top, halfway back along the body. From this position he could control the engine with his left hand, the rudder with his right hand and the stabilisation of the wings with his feet. The craft was equipped with two bicycle wheels and a roller on a frame for landing and support of the craft on the ground.

More pioneering designs

As more aviators took to the air, and aeroplanes began to prove more feasible as a means of transport, there were those who set out to make their flying machines smaller and smaller. In 1907, Alberto Santos-Dumont, a wealthy Brazilian living in Paris, began producing a series of aircraft called the Demoiselles, reckoned to be the smallest in the world. Not only that, but plans for building your own Demoiselle were soon advertised for members of the public who, for the price of $2, could attempt to build their own flying machine. The advertisements claimed: 'The machine is unencumbered by patent rights, the famous aviator preferring to place his invention at the disposal of the world in the interest of the art to which he has devoted his life.' Each set of plans comprised seven blueprints, showing construction details and descriptions of how to complete the building.

Not long after, Santos-Dumont's record for building the smallest aircraft was broken by another French aviator named Raoul Vendome, who built a one-man aeroplane with a seat between the wings. The craft was only 16 feet long, 16 feet wide and weighed a mere 180 pounds, and could easily be lifted by one man.

Working Drawings of the "Demoiselle"

Price $2⁰⁰ Postpaid

SANTOS-DUMONT'S
Remarkable Aeroplane

The Smallest Flyer Ever Built

One of the Most Successful

Complete plans for the construction of the wonderful monoplane offered to the public for the first time.

The machine is unencumbered by patent rights, the famous aviator preferring to place his invention at the disposal of the world in the interest of the art to which he has devoted his life.   These plans were secured by representatives of Popular Mechanics from Santos-Dumont, and are the result of consultations with his engineers and observations made at his workshops.

How the "DEMOISELLE" Ranks With Other Machines

From New York Times, October 9, 1910.

"M. Garros, famous French aviator, uses a Demoiselle aeroplane, the invention of Santos-Dumont, which has proved to be one of the most interesting types of flying machines in Europe. It has been called the humming bird of the heavier-than-air brood. It is the smallest flying machine in existence, weighing less than 250 pounds. It is capable of enormous speed, and darts about through the air in a way that has provoked both laughter and wonderment from the crowds at the European meetings. Garros is by far the most expert driver of these little machines in Europe. During the past season he has made remarkable flights in various places, but his flights from Pinard to St. Malo, over the water, have been regarded as most remarkable. While these baby monoplanes in the hands of ordinary pilots keep very close to the ground, Garros has driven his machine to great altitudes, and has taken his place in many of the important contests of France with the larger monoplanes."

The set comprises seven large blue prints, showing every detail of construction, accompanied by a description of how to build.

POPULAR MECHANICS COMPANY
318 W. Washington Street, CHICAGO, ILLINOIS

An advertisement for building your own Demoiselle plane.

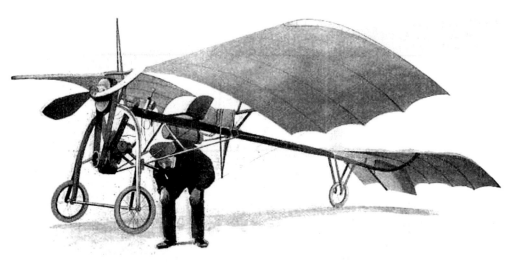

Vendome's aircraft, small and light enough to be lifted by a man.

A German designed pigmy plane in the 1920s held no passengers, just a single pilot who lay down along the length of the miniature fuselage to handle the controls.

The early years of the twentieth century were rampant with strange designs of aeroplane, some of which were successful, many of which never proceeded beyond a designer's drawing board. They included examples such as what the French called the Phantom Aeroplane, a curious many-winged craft multiplane that was among the first to include a hood, made of mica, to protect the pilot from the elements aloft.

Around the same time, a plane made of wood was exhibited at an air show in Paris. Apart from the wooden construction, its prime unusual feature was a turbine at the front in place of a propeller. Not unlike the jet engines that would follow in

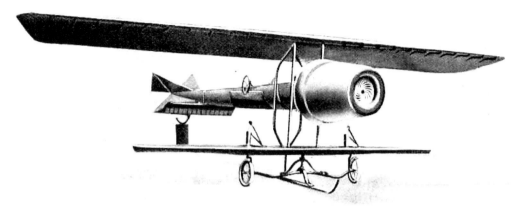

An aircraft that used a turbo in place of a propeller.

later years, this sucked in air at the front and expelled it at the rear, thus forcing the machine forwards through the air.

There were even plans around this time for early forms of helicopter, notably one from Otto Luyties, the son of a German immigrant to America and a graduate of the Massachusetts Institute of Technology. Launching his career as an engineer in 1900, he set out to develop plans for a helicopter, which he considered to be a much neglected form of transport, very much overshadowed by the rise in popularity of the aeroplane. By 1908 he had a working model, which he demonstrated on open land near Baltimore.

This strange craft had eight rotating blades 35 feet in diameter and made of light canvas stretched between steel tubing. They were attached to concentric steel shafts that allowed them to rotate in opposite directions at up to eighty-one revolutions per minute. The motive power came from an air-cooled eight-cylinder motor, the

The Luyties working model of a primitive helicopter.

whole thing mounted on a platform on which the pilot sat with the blades above him like a gigantic umbrella.

During the tests, high winds repeatedly wrecked the machine, which had to be repaired on the spot before resuming the tests that were carried out preparatory to building the helicopter proper. The tests were moderately successful, but when a final windstorm wrecked the machine for the last time, further construction was curtailed through lack of funds.

Luyties, however, gained much information from the tests and, in *Scientific American* magazine of 11 July 1908, he published the results with elaborate recommendations for other experimenters interested in the construction of a helicopter style of flying machine.

Aero-hydroplanes

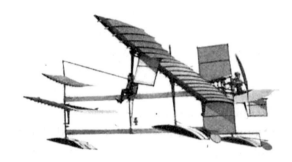

The aero-hydroplane in flight (above) and its sad ending in the water (below).

The Curtiss hydroplane in action.

In 1911, an aero-hydroplane was entered into motorboat exhibition races at Monaco. Despite partaking in the motorboat section of the event, the craft was more of a plane than a boat, as was demonstrated when it took off from the water and sailed into the air. In fact, it made several successful flights before the one that ended with a too sudden landing on the water, which resulted in the half-boat, half-aircraft breaking in half. The pilot got a soaking but was otherwise unhurt.

Hydroplane development continued in France and America. American Glenn Curtiss continued work on his own designs of aero-hydroplanes that could take off or land on both land and water, where their speed was said to outstrip fast motorboats. Curtiss's design used a pontoon-like float in the centre of the machine and cylindrical floats on the wing tips to steady the craft if it tilted on water.

Two 1912 airshows

By the start of the second decade of the twentieth century there were few who doubted that, as a means of transport, the aeroplane was here to stay. An exhibition staged by French aeroplane manufacturers and reviewed in *Popular Mechanics* magazine of March 1912 reported:

Staged under the dome of the Grand Palais in Paris were ranged stand after stand of wonderful devices of steel, wood, wire and fabric fashioned by human ingenuity into cunning semblances of nature's transportation, the bird. Almost all the machines shown were capable of flight, all represent distinct improvement towards some unknown future perfection, and most are now capable of practical military and commercial use.

The most conspicuous feature of this latest form of aviation is the almost total neglect of the dirigible. Gigantic gas bags were conspicuous by their absence. In the place of these, there reigned supreme the proved flying machine of today and the developing device of tomorrow – the aeroplane – almost every model in the building being the creation of a far-seeing, technically able and well-financed concern, seriously and successfully engaged in the commercial exploitation of a new field of engineering, on which great successes have been achieved and in which even greater are coming. Not only were most of the machines shown capable of flight, many of them had actually flown.

Probably the most important technical development in evidence was the thoroughly emphasised trend toward the use of streamline forms as a means of reducing the forward resistance of the aeroplane and therefore the amount of power required for its propulsion. Another important development is the increasing use of metal in place of wood.

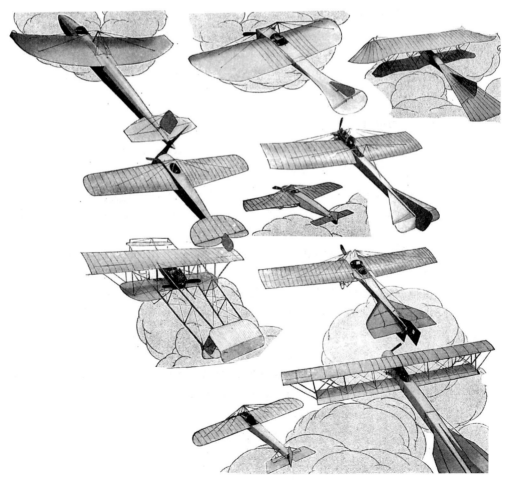

Artist's impression of some of the aircraft on show at a Paris airshow in 1912.

The Bullet, a streamlined aircraft on show in New York in 1912.

The same year, at New York's Grand Central Palace, America staged its first aero show. Among the new designs of aircraft, streamlining was also much to the fore, as seen in craft like the Bullet, which featured a blunt nose at the front and a propeller at the rear. Other exhibits illustrated new refinements in aircraft, together with increased strength of their structure. Hydro-planes also caused much interest and speculation that flying would soon become a major sport in the country.

Steam-powered flight

In 1913, the *Daily Mail* newspaper in England offered a prize of £10,000 to the first person to fly from North America to the UK, or vice versa, in seventy-two continuous hours. There were many who planned such a flight, including a French law student from Chicago who set out to build a steam-powered aircraft for the task.

The machine planned claimed to have the widest wingspan ever made, 100 feet 6 inches from tip to tip, and constructed from aluminium. The motive power was two steam turbines fuelled by coke. Each engine ran 8-foot propellers, two at the front of the craft and two at the rear. Six square shutters in the wings were designed to open and close as needed to help control stability. The machine was planned to carry a crew of six together with their provisions for the Atlantic trip, 800 pounds of coke and 500 gallons of water in two boilers, all of which the inventor claimed would keep his aircraft in the air for fifty-eight hours.

Needless to say, even if the machine was ever built, it never flew across the Atlantic. The *Daily Mail* prize was eventually claimed in 1919 by British aviators John Alcock and Arthur Brown.

The steam-powered aircraft planned to fly the Atlantic.

The flying tea tray

The flying tea tray with its ring-like wings.

Experiments in England in 1914 resulted in a strange craft with wings that curved backwards to meet an enlarged tail, thus forming a complete circular ring. The idea was that if the craft capsized, the wings would help it to automatically right itself. The body, which was little more than that of a conventional monoplane aircraft of the day, extended through the centre of the ring with which it joined at either side of the rim. While still in its experimental stages the craft was said to have made several successful flights. Its shape earned it the title of the flying tea tray.

The helicopter balloon

A French idea for combining a dirigible with a helicopter made its first flights in 1921. It consisted of a framework in which the pilot sat between winglike structures that held the helicopter propellers, while a long, tubular-shaped balloon floated above. Lift was provided by the propellers, while the balloon helped to stabilise the machine once in the air. The inventor claimed that the propellers were designed on what he called a recovery of energy principle, inspired by the endurance of birds on 1,000-mile migration flights. The propellers proved to be about 20 per cent more efficient than some of the more recognised types without any assistance from the balloon needed for lifting the machine off the ground.

How a French inventor combined an early helicopter design with a balloon.

Planes with parachutes

The safety of air travel took a step forward in 1921 with the invention of a parachute capable of supporting the entire passenger compartment of an aircraft. The idea was that if an aeroplane got into trouble, the pilot pulled a lever which released a small parachute. As that small parachute opened its pull released a slightly larger one. The pull of the two combined then released a third even larger parachute and it was this that lifted the entire passenger cabin out of the disabled aircraft's fuselage. As the plane went on to presumably crash-land somewhere, the parachute lowered the passenger cabin safely to the ground.

How the entire cabin of an aircraft might descend to earth on a parachute in the event of engine failure.

Later, in 1926, passengers nervous of crashing might have taken reassurance from the invention of the biggest parachute made up until that time. It was attached, not to any of the passengers or even to just the cabin, but to the aeroplane itself. During its first test the parachute safely landed a stalled plane from a height of 2,500 feet in 66 seconds. The parachute was designed by Harry Doucett, a chief petty officer in the US Navy. It was fastened to the plane with 40 feet of steel cable and carried, when folded, in a compartment beneath the fuselage at the back of the pilot's seat. The pilot had only to pull a lever which broke the light twine that attached it to the plane. When released, the cables pulled the parachute into position above the plane, where it inflated.

Possibly the world's largest parachute, made to save a light aircraft from crashing.

The Air Sedan

Billed as a tandem-plane that would revolutionise flying, the Air Sedan, which made an appearance in 1921, was designed to be safer than other aircraft. Its design meant that, in the event of an engine failure in mid-air, the aircraft could drift gently to the ground. Two leading car manufacturers in America showed an interest in building the car-like plane, but its inventor died even before its maiden flight.

The evolutionary Air Sedan, which failed to make its way into the history books.

A giant triplane

Gianni Caproni, an Italian aerial engineer, designed one of the most gigantic heavier-than-air machines ever built, up until the time of its launch in 1921. Called the *Epocha*, and weighing about 25 tons when fully loaded, it consisted of three independent triplanes attached to the fuselage in tandem. It took off and landed over water. No less than eight 12-cylinder, 400-horsepower engines drove independent propellers, although they were only used all at the same time during take-off and in case of emergencies. Once airborne, some of the engines were held in reserve, using first one group, then the other. Four engines were mounted on the centre wing of each of the three triplanes, three propellers at the front of the wing and the fourth at the rear. The 66-foot fuselage of the huge plane seated 100 passengers with baggage. Sleeping births folded up into the upper sides of the body and, when lowered, hung crosswise to the cabin.

Until 1921, Gianni Caproni's triplane was one of biggest heavier-than-air machines ever built.

Built on the shores of Italy's Lake Maggiore, *Epocha* made two successful flights in March 1921, although it was slightly damaged during the second flight's landing, and then further damaged when a storm swept the area a little later. Undeterred, Caproni set out to reconstruct the gigantic aircraft, with a vision of it carrying its passengers on nonstop 1,000-mile trips. His ultimate plan was for a fleet of similarly designed but even bigger aircraft capable of carrying 300 or more passengers on transatlantic voyages lasting twenty-four hours or even less.

Planes inside planes

In the early 1920s a plan was announced by a Russian-German combine to provide air passengers with a means of leaving an aeroplane without it having to land. The proposal was for large non-stop express planes to incorporate smaller gliders

A German idea for a plane that incorporated a small glider that allowed passengers to disembark mid-flight.

within their holds. When a destination for disembarking was being approached, the aircrew would unfold a small so-called air-boat from the hold and lower it to dangle on wires beneath the larger aircraft. Passengers would then descend from the large plane and buckle themselves into the small craft below. The larger craft that the passengers had just left would slow and the pilot of the smaller craft would pull a lever to disengage it from the plane above, whereupon it would glide to a safe landing below. There is no evidence to suggest the plans ever came to fruition.

The autogyrator

The autogyrator, built by a Spanish inventor in 1925, was a cross between an aeroplane and a helicopter. The aircraft began life as a biplane, from which the two top wings were removed to be replaced with four revolving blades like those on a helicopter. Unlike a traditional helicopter, however, there was no power applied to these blades; they were simply allowed to revolve freely like the sails of a windmill, except of course that they were arranged horizontally rather than vertically. The aircraft's engine rotated a front-mounted propeller and this was used to propel the plane along a runway in the usual way. The rush of air that resulted from the plane's dash along the runway then began to turn the blades on the top. When they reached approximately eighty revolutions per minute they exerted a lifting power that helped the plane take off. Once in the air, it handled like a traditional aeroplane. The advantage over a more traditional aircraft was the way in which the revolving blades aided landing and also prevented a serious crash if the craft happened to stall at low heights.

The autogyrator, which was like a cross between an aeroplane and a helicopter.

Giant transatlantic aircraft

A huge German aircraft planned for transatlantic flights with passenger cabins in its wings.

In 1926, German inventor Walter G. Brenner prepared plans for a giant seaplane for transatlantic flights, in which the passengers would travel in cabins situated in the huge wings, with glass windows at their leading edges. The crew, freight space and room for more passengers would also be carried in the plane's fuselage, which was shaped more like the hull of a boat. The aircraft was designed to fly at high altitudes of between 26,000 and 33,000 feet, where it was estimated lower wind resistance would allow speeds of up to 250 miles per hour. It was acknowledged that at such heights passengers, as well as the engines, would need to have air supplied by pumps to give a pressure equal to that at sea level. The plane would therefore need to be airtight. The fuselage would also be equipped with winglike pontoons on each side to give support on the surface of water from where the aircraft would take off and land. Brenner estimated that when flying at high altitudes, lower wind resistance would mean the two engines at the front and one at the back needed to be no larger than those found in more conventional aircraft and that fuel consumption would also be economical.

The Sea Flea

A strange craft, half boat, half aeroplane and called the Sea Flea, was built in 1927 for a flight across the Atlantic. The strange looking craft was designed not to fly at high altitudes, but rather to skim close to the surface of the water. Since it was also

The Sea Flea: half plane, half boat.

designed to float, there was no fear of forced landings. It was claimed that the Sea Flea could reach speeds of 75 miles per hour. In tests it travelled across the English Channel from England to France, carrying a pilot and three passengers, in just twenty-six minutes.

The Sky Diner

A tri-motor Fokker aeroplane of the late 1920s became dubbed the Sky Diner because of its luxurious cabin. Here passengers could enjoy all the conveniences of a plush pullman car on the railways. The seats were like luxurious armchairs arranged around tables where meals were served by waiters fresh from a galley where they were cooked. Anything from a light lunch to a five-course meal could be prepared on a small electric cooker. The luxury cabin also incorporated a writing desk, a toilet and ample space for passenger luggage. Smoking was permitted. Cruising at between 5,000 and 10,000 feet, the Sky Diner's chef had to be aware of the way the boiling point of water varied with altitude. Passengers were therefore asked to keep this in mind in case their eggs turned out not to have been boiled to the degree they expected.

The Comet Plane

Not all aeroplanes had wings. The Comet Plane, which was tested in 1930, resembled a barrel, open at both ends, with a propeller inside a wire cage at the front. It worked like a box kite. Air sucked in at the front and expelled from the rear caused it to rise in the air, when a large rudder on the rear helped it to steer. The unusual aircraft could take off from land or water and, being wingless, could easily be stored in a normal car garage. Its German inventor claimed it would reach 300 miles per hour and planned to fly it from New York to Berlin in twelve hours.

The Flying Duck

Plans for a gigantic aeroplane to be built in Germany in 1932 saw a revolutionary design that was dominated by one enormous wing that housed the passengers. Entry into the aircraft was via a stairway leading into the wing. Inside, there were cabins

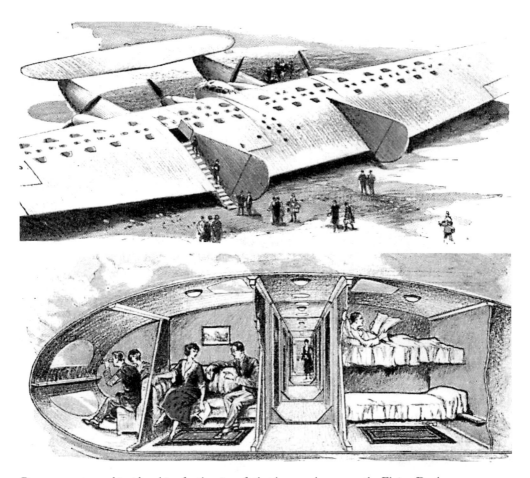

Passenger entry and inside cabins for the aircraft that became known as the Flying Duck.

where passengers could sit or take in the view from the side of the wing, while across a narrow corridor there were sleeping cabins. The craft's undercarriage was designed to be drawn up into the craft once airborne. Officially called the J-1000, the aircraft took on the nickname of the Flying Duck because of its appearance to the bird in flight.

Tailless plane

Flying was said to have been made virtually foolproof, eliminating pilot errors for good, thanks to a new kind of tailless aeroplane invented in England in 1926. Instead of the traditional fuselage tipped with rudders and elevators, the new kind of craft had a much shortened body ending in a propeller and a huge wing that swept back over the entire body, much like the wing of a bird. The advantage over

The tailless aeroplane was said to eliminate pilot errors.

more traditionally designed aircraft was said to be that it would remain stable in any flying altitude, whether on a straight course or when steeply climbing, a manoeuvre in which the wings of ordinary aircraft might lose lifting power and so lead to the engine stalling. Landing was by way of two wheels at the front and a third at the rear of the body.

Flying wing

Konrad Kraft's flying wing aircraft, defined by its W-shaped wings.

If plans by German engineer Konrad Kraft had been fully realised, the design of passenger aircraft might have taken a completely new turn. His idea was for aircraft wings to be shaped like the letter 'W', with the fuselage in the centre and landing wheels in the lower angles of the odd-shaped wings.

In 1936, Kraft built a model with a wingspan of 6 feet 6 inches, which proved his plane needed less space than normal to take off and that the angular shape of the wings meant the craft was unaffected by side winds. Had his ideas come to fruition the next step would have been for a full-size plane with 'W'-shaped wings, a passenger compartment between them and fuel tanks in the hull.

Jellyfish plane

Vertical lift-off in a craft that moved like a jellyfish was proposed in 1936. The inventor was John Domenjoz from New York, whose previous plans had included an aircraft with a sail mounted above it like a yacht to enable it to move through the air.

His jellyfish aircraft consisted of a one-man machine powered by a petrol engine and with a large circular flexible canopy mounted above it on metal frames. A

The plane designed to move through the air like a jellyfish moves through water.

crank and piston rod from the engine drove a centre section of the canopy in an up-and-down motion, while a complicated set of valves in the centre of the canopy controlled the air pressure as it moved in its downward direction. As a result, the strange craft was said to be able to lift from the ground and travel through the air in much the way that a jellyfish moves through water. The top of the canopy was also equipped with a parachute to help the craft descend and land.

Vertical take-off

Vertical take-off became a popular concept in the 1920s and 1930s.

The 1920s through to the 1930s saw a fad for aircraft that replaced traditional wings with huge rotating wings above the cockpit, driven by the same engine that turned the machine's propeller. The result was a craft that was half aeroplane and half helicopter. An experimental machine tested in 1931 ascended vertically before flying in a straight line, and then descended with the power off as the whirling wings acted like a parachute.

A new era

In 1939, the Second World War broke out. In the almost unbelievably brief thirty-six years between then and the first manned flight, aeroplane design and air travel had come a very long way. Now, with supremacy in the air being more important than ever, the design of new aircraft became necessarily more serious and new designs far more practical, though for the next few years, more for military purposes than for pleasure-seeking civilian passengers. When the world emerged from the war in 1945, the design of aircraft had entered a new era. Air travel had come of age. The brief era of wild speculation, adventurous experimentation, strange ideas and what often proved to be impossible ways to construct weird and wonderful flying machines was over.

Picture Credits

Many of the pictures in this book were taken from vintage copies of *Popular Mechanics* magazine, dated between 1904 and 1930. Although their age places them in the public domain, they had previously been gathered together electronically by James Kirk, who was then entitled to claim copyright on the issues and contents. I am, therefore, very grateful to James for giving me permission to use these pictures in my book.

Cover pictures: Lower left, from an original painting by Richard Shaw; all other pictures from various vintage issues of *Popular Mechanics* magazine.

Internal pages containing pictures from issues of *Popular Mechanics*, dated between 1904 and 1930, are as follows. Pages: vii, 1, 7 (upper and lower left), 34, 36, 47, 52 (lower), 54, 57, 60, 61, 64, 71, 72 (upper and lower), 74, 80 (upper), 83, 84–6, 88–102, 106–108, 113, 120–3, 128–41, 143–4, 146, 150–4, 157–9, 164–87, 190.

Other picture credits are as follows:

Page 2:	Internet Archive Book Images, via Wikimedia Commons.
Page 3:	Courtesy of the United States Patent and Trademark Office.
Page 4:	From *Scientific American*, c1890.
Page 4:	Courtesy of the United States Patent and Trademark Office.
Page 5:	Public Domain. University of Southern California Libraries and California Historical Society.
Page 6:	From *Popular Science*, c1915.
Page 6:	From *Le Petit Journal*, December 1924.
Page 7:	From *Modern Mechanix*, May 1930 (lower right).
Page 8:	Автор фото неизвестен. Public domain via Wikimedia Commons.
Page 9:	From *Die Wolchenschay*, January 1920, courtesy of Feòrag Forsyth.
Page 10:	From *Railway Wonders of the World*, issue 25.
Page 11:	Courtesy of the United States Patent and Trademark Office.
Page 12:	© Feòrag Forsyth.
Page 13:	Courtesy of East Dunbartonshire Leisure & Culture Trust Archives and Local Studies.
Page 14:	From *Railways Wonders of the World*, issue 17.
Page 15:	From *Railways Wonders of the World*, issue 17 (upper); courtesy of *Newsquest Herald and Times* (lower).
Page 16:	Unknown author, public domain.
Page 17:	Courtesy of East Dunbartonshire Leisure & Culture Trust Archives and Local Studies (upper); attributed to Richard Sutcliffe via Wikimedia Commons (lower).

Page 18:   From *The Pneumatic Despatch*, 1868.
Page 20:   From *The Illustrated London News*, 1864.
Page 22:   From *The Engineer*, 1877.
Page 24:   From *The Pictorial Times*, 1845.
Page 25:   Rosser 1954 / CC BY-SA, via Wikimedia Commons (upper); from *The Pictorial Times*, 1845 (lower).
Page 26:   Otto Spamer/public domain, via Wikimedia Commons.
Page 27:   Courtesy of Exeter Memories.
Page 28:   From a contemporary postcard.
Page 30:   From a contemporary postcard.
Page 31:   From a contemporary postcard (upper); courtesy of the Grange Museum, Rottingdean (lower).
Page 32:   From the Douglas d'Enno collection.
Page 33:   © John Wade.
Page 38:   From *Scientific American*, 1870.
Pages 39–44:   From *Appletons' Journal*, 1878.
Page 42:   Public domain.
Pages 43–5:   From *Appletons' Journal*, 1878.
Page 46:   John S. Johnston, public domain.
Page 48:   From *The Illustrated London News*, June 1850.
Page 49:   From a contemporary postcard.
Page 50:   From *Modern Mechanix*.
Page 51:   From *Railway Wonders of the World* (upper and lower).
Page 52:   Courtesy of the United States Patent and Trademark Office (upper).
Page 53:   Courtesy of the United States Patent and Trademark Office (upper); Wikimedia Commons (lower).
Page 55:   From *Railway Wonders of the World* (upper and lower).
Page 58:   Public domain.
Page 59:   From *Scientific American*, 1866.
Page 63:   Courtesy of the United States Patent and Trademark Office.
Page 65:   From a Rauch & Lang Carriage Company advertisement, public domain via Wikimedia Commons.
Page 66:   From *Sunset Magazine*, 1913, public domain via Wikimedia Commons.
Page 67:   Unknown author, public domain via Wikimedia Commons.
Page 68:   Public domain via Wikimedia Commons.
Page 70:   Public domain via Wikimedia Commons.
Page 73:   Public domain, via Wikimedia Commons.
Pages 75–6:   © Steve Beamish.
Page 78:   From *The Engineer*, 1869.

Page 79:   From *Brockhaus' Conversations-Lexikon*, 1887.

Page 80:   From *Century Magazine*, 1890 (lower).

Page 81:   From an original poster by Karl Edwards (upper); from *The Tricyclists' Indispensible Annual* and Handbook, 1883 (lower).

Page 82:   From *Silber & Fleming Catalogue*, 1885, via Wikimedia Commons.

Page 87:   From *Modern Mechanix*, 1939.

Page 104:   From *Modern Mechanix*, 1936.

Page 105:   From *Modern Mechanix*, 1936.

Pages 108–109:   From *Mechanics and Handicraft*, 1936.

Page 110:   Public domain, photographer unknown.

Page 111:   From *Mechanics and Handicraft*, 1935.

Page 112:   Starysatyr / CC BY-SA via Wikimedia Commons.

Page 114:   Parsons, Public domain, via Wikimedia Commons.

Page 115:   © John Wade.

Pages 116–18:   From *The Illustrated London News*, 1859.

Page 119:   National Maritime Museum, Public domain, via Wikimedia Commons.

Page 120:   From a contemporary postcard (upper).

Page 125:   Courtesy of the United States Patent and Trademark Office.

Page 126:   From a contemporary French postcard by Marius Bar.

Page 127:   World Imaging via Wikimedia Commons.

Page 142:   From *Modern Mechanix*.

Page 145:   From *The Graphic*, 1877.

Page 147:   Courtesy of the United States Patent and Trademark Office.

Page 148:   Woodcut from a nineteenth-century French magazine.

Page 149:   © Ron Holloway.

Page 150:   USN Public domain via Wikimedia Commons (upper).

Page 155:   Associated Press Oakland Tribune. Public domain via Wikimedia Common (upper); The National Archives UK. Public domain via Wikimedia Commons (lower).

Page 156:   Gus Pasquarella. Public domain via Wikimedia Commons.

Page 160:   © Ron Holloway (upper).

Page 160:   Courtesy of the United States Patent and Trademark Office (lower).

Pages 161–3:   © Ron Holloway.

Page 167:   C.C. Pierce & Co. Public domain (lower).

Page 173:   From *Scientific American*.

Page 188:   From *Modern Mechanix*, 1936.

Page 189:   From *Modern Mechanix*, 1936.

Index